PRAISE FOR *BOSS UP!*

AF270905

"Lindsay Teague Moreno is a no-fluff, no-fear leader for entrepreneurs. This book is the perfect guide to starting a business and fulfilling your dreams."

—John C. Maxwell, #1 *New York Times* bestselling author and world-renowned leadership expert

"*Boss Up!* should be mandatory reading for every female entrepreneur. It's what you wish your girlfriend had told you about what it takes and what to expect as a mom, wife, and badass business owner. Lindsay's relatable humor will have you laughing while you lap up invaluable lessons on mind-set and strategy and the skills you need to kill in business without the guilt."

—Chalene Johnson, *New York Times* bestselling author and business and lifestyle expert

"Lindsay combines both heartfelt vulnerability with no-nonsense practicality in a way that speaks to today's female business owner. She makes not-so-sexy topics, like finding your niche, standard operating procedures, and managing a team, feel fun and doable. As an artist, I could've used a book like this five years ago when I was just starting out. This is the book I needed then, and it's what I need now as I continue to be a leader in my industry."

—Amira Rahim, Better Than Art School creator

"You will absolutely snort-laugh and definitely ugly-cry while learning these actionable, no-BS lessons for building a killer business—and becoming a better you while you do it. You've been warned y'all!"

—Kelsey Humphreys, author and motivational comedian

"Lindsay cuts through the crap and gets to the heart of what it takes to be a successful entrepreneur. This book will guide you through building an effective business the same way your mom guided you through life—with love, support, and a healthy kick in the butt when you need it."

—Elizabeth Giorgi, Emmy Award winner and Mighteor Studios founder

"*Boss Up!* is the guide I wish I'd had when starting my own business. Lindsay delivers hard-nosed business advice while making you laugh out loud with the realities of being both a mom and entrepreneur. With contagious enthusiasm and practical tips, this is the book to read if you want to grow your business."

—Tonya Dalton, author, *The Joy of Missing Out*, and
inkWELL Press Productivity Co. CEO

"In an age when it's easy to call yourself an entrepreneur, here is a book that tells you the truth about the hard, beautiful, rewarding work of owning a business. *Boss Up!* is the most practical guide to running a business I have ever read; every woman should read it."

—Jeff Goins, bestselling author, *The Art of Work*

"*Boss Up!* will make you laugh, cry, and then you'll want to get out and hustle! As a fellow stay-at-home mom turned business owner, this book feels like home! Lindsay gets it. Tried and true. *Boss Up!* will give you the permission to get out there and fuel the fire that is already burning within you!"

—Chari Pack, Persnickety Prints founder

"My only complaint with Lindsay's book is that I didn't have it when I started my business seven years ago. Lindsay has the sharp mind of a woman who means business but the heart and humor of a friend you want to talk to for hours. As an entrepreneur who doesn't have kids, I do want them in my future, and reading *Boss Up!* left me optimistic, not with it being just an option but a wonderful option for me."

—Jess Ekstrom, Headbands of Hope founder and author, *Chasing the Bright Side*

"You think you know what to expect from business books? Think again! Lindsay breaks the business book mold with *Boss Up!* She'll have you simultaneously laughing and learning with her no-nonsense humorous approach. Lindsay's entrepreneurial success is impressive, but even more impressive is her ability to share those lessons with others."

—Carrie Colbert, entrepreneur and investor

"Lindsay knows what she's doing, and her energy and enthusiasm come through on every page. *Boss Up!* will make you want to get up and go!"

—Elise Blaha Cripe, author, *Big Dreams, Daily Joys*, Get to Work Book creator

"For the seven years I've known Lindsay professionally, I've always been deeply inspired by her passion for helping women find their life purpose. She shows women around the world, regardless of circumstances, that with the right tools, perspective, and personal authenticity, they, too, can be successful in every aspect of life. *Boss Up!* is another fantastic example of her dedication to momtrepreneurs everywhere. If you're interested in building a business, growing your profile as a thought leader, or just need some motivation in life, do yourself a huge favor and read this book."

—Jared Turner, entrepreneur and Young Living Essential Oils president

"*Boss Up!* is a fantastic, straight-talking road map for getting started and for continuing to evolve and thrive as a woman entrepreneur. Lindsay takes the lessons she's learned through her own experience and shares them in an honest, humorous, and inspiring way. *Boss Up!* will make you want to dive right in and take the next steps forward no matter where you are in the process."

—Ali Edwards, business owner, AliEdwards.com

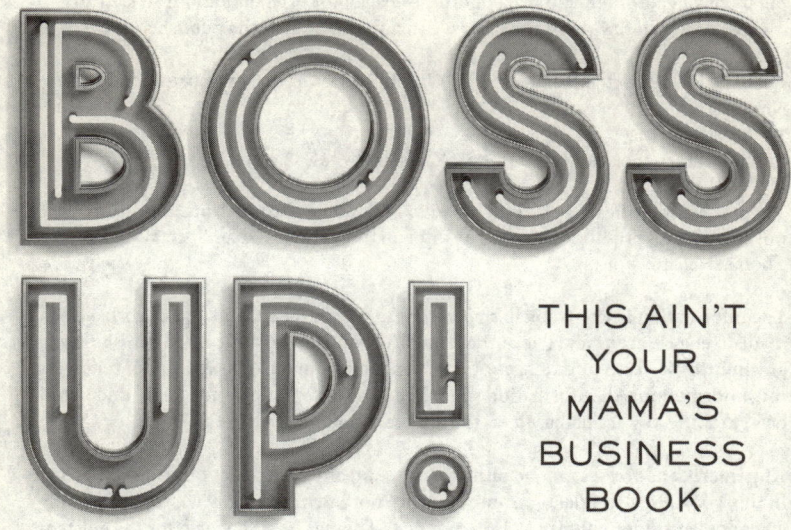

BOSS UP!

THIS AIN'T YOUR MAMA'S BUSINESS BOOK

LINDSAY TEAGUE MORENO

W PUBLISHING GROUP

AN IMPRINT OF THOMAS NELSON

© 2019 LTM Consulting, LLC

All rights reserved. No portion of this book may be reproduced, stored in a retrieval system, or transmitted in any form or by any means—electronic, mechanical, photocopy, recording, scanning, or other—except for brief quotations in critical reviews or articles, without the prior written permission of the publisher.

Published in Nashville, Tennessee, by W Publishing Group, an imprint of Thomas Nelson.

Published in association with Yates & Yates, www.yates2.com.

Thomas Nelson titles may be purchased in bulk for educational, business, fundraising, or sales promotional use. For information, please e-mail SpecialMarkets@ ThomasNelson.com.

The information in this book has been carefully researched, and all efforts have been made to ensure accuracy. The authors and the publisher assume no responsibility for any injuries suffered or damages or losses incurred during or as a result of following this information. All information should be carefully studied and clearly understood before taking any action based on the information or advice in this book.

Any Internet addresses, phone numbers, or company or product information printed in this book are offered as a resource and are not intended in any way to be or to imply an endorsement by Thomas Nelson, nor does Thomas Nelson vouch for the existence, content, or services of these sites, phone numbers, companies, or products beyond the life of this book.

ISBN 978-0-7852-2442-6 (TP)
ISBN 978-0-7852-3011-3 (IE)

Library of Congress Cataloging-in-Publication Data

Names: Moreno, Lindsay Teague, 1980– author.
Title: Boss up! : this ain't your mama's business book / Lindsay Teague Moreno.
Description: Nashville, Tennessee : W Publishing Group, [2019] | Includes
  bibliographical references. |
Identifiers: LCCN 2019009000 (print) | LCCN 2019010746 (ebook) |
  ISBN 9780785224433 (E-book) | ISBN 9780785224419 (hardcover)
Subjects: LCSH: Success in business. | Entrepreneurship. | Businesswomen—United
  States.
Classification: LCC HF5386 (ebook) | LCC HF5386 .M757 2019 (print) |
  DDC 658.0082—dc23
LC record available at https://lccn.loc.gov/2019009000

Printed in the United States of America

21 22 23 24 25 LSC 10 9 8 7 6 5 4 3 2 1

To my husband, Michael.

*My ten-year-old self knew this book
would be a reality one day, but
she could never have predicted a love like
ours. It takes a special man
to support me the way you do. Every ten-
year-old girl should dream bigger
about the kind of love that's available to her.*

CONTENTS

FOREWORD

The first time I met Lindsay Teague Moreno was in a field somewhere in the middle of Utah.

I was surrounded by snow-covered mountains, the kinds of horses you think exist only in movies, and hundreds of fancy tents.

In the center stood Lindsay, smiling and laughing amid the kindest audience I'd ever met. She created the event to teach a few hundred friends how she built her wildly successful business and thought it would be fun to "Hustle Under the Stars."

I thought I was there to teach, but I was wrong. I was there to learn.

There's just something different about Lindsay.

Have you ever been around people like that?

They see the world as an adventure. They see challenges as opportunities. They see horizons as invitations.

And the best part is they dare you to take the journey with them.

Fast forward a few years. I'm no longer in Utah. Now I'm sitting in Lindsay's living room, discussing my new book, *Finish*, with her and her husband, Michael. I speak and write for a living, so the release of a new book is a big moment for my business. As I am prone to do, I turned to Lindsay for some advice.

She gave me great feedback, including many of the ideas you'll find in this book, and then she called me out of my comfort zone.

"Let's do a Facebook Live right now about your new book."

I was a little hesitant. It wasn't for sale yet; it didn't even have a cover. Have you ever been apprehensive about your business idea? Maybe you thought it wasn't ready for the light of day yet. Maybe you've been sitting quietly on a secret what-if idea for years. Then you better watch out about being around Lindsay. She's going to convince you to launch.

She talked me into it, and that night, after a short Facebook Live with her audience, my book became the fastest mover and shaker on Amazon. Presales skyrocketed. My publisher was stunned. "What happened last night?" they asked.

"Lindsay happened," I said, marveling at her ability to build her own business audience and then the generosity to share it with me.

The generosity should not have surprised me. I once checked into my hotel for one of Lindsay's events, and in my room were 150 presents perfectly displayed on the couch. As a surprise, months before the event, she had asked attendees to bring a special item from their home states for me. I was overwhelmed but, because I travel a lot, instantly thought, *How am I going to get all of this home?*

Then I looked at the mountain of presents a little closer. They were sitting in the world's largest Tumi suitcase. Lindsay had already thought through every detail of this moment, which is what smart business leaders always do.

When I say that Lindsay is great at building a business, I think back to that event in Utah.

When I say that Lindsay is great at creating an audience and a platform, I think back to that night she blew up my book in a matter of minutes.

When I say that Lindsay approaches life with an infectious sense of fun, I think back to that hotel room overflowing with unexpected gifts.

There are a lot of people who write motivational books. There are a lot of people who write business books. There aren't a lot of people who have actually built something that redefines an industry and then are kind enough to explain what they did.

That's what Lindsay does.

It's why I keep asking her for advice. It's why I keep speaking at her events. It's why I told her this book needed to exist years ago when it was just an idea.

You might not be standing in a field in Utah right now, though I wish you were because you wouldn't believe how majestic those horses are. I'm pretty sure that farm had unicorns.

You might be ten years down the road with your business or ten minutes into a brand-new idea.

You might know exactly what you want to do or haven't got a clue, except for a persistent belief that there's a business in your future.

Regardless of where you are right now, I know where you're about to be.

In Lindsay's world.

It's bright. It's honest. It's fun. It's creative. And it's going to do more for your business than you can possibly imagine.

Get ready to boss up.

—JON ACUFF
New York Times bestselling author and speaker

Introduction

WHY IS NOBODY ELSE LOSING IT?

I find myself in the middle of one of my real-life nightmares: sitting on an airplane while it bounces wildly through the air. The pilot might call it "light turbulence," but I call it a preplunge warning.

Flight attendants walk surefooted up and down the aisles, smiling through what has to be a prelude to certain death. The walking doesn't help me. In my brain it's like adding a pack of wild dogs into a room of screaming toddlers. Panic. Make it stop.

I've got to figure out how I'm going to explain this to my five-year-old sitting next to me. How do you explain, "Prepare for riding a fireball toward planet earth" to her? She's watching *Minions* on my iPad, blissfully unaware, and downing boxes of orange Tic Tacs like it's a sport.

The flight attendants are trying to serve me food. *Food? At a time like this?* I can't eat this bag of pretzel mix. What do you think this is? A party?

I ask myself, *Why is nobody else losing it?*

This is my life each and every time there is so much as a turn in an airplane. My husband, Michael, and I flew more than two hundred thousand miles last year. You can imagine how much he loves working on the road with me. He always looks at me like I'm out of my mind, saying things that don't even help a tiny bit—like "It's fine" or "Stop" or "Calm down"—while I grip my seat as if my hands were the jaws of life.*

I started my first business five years ago and, within months, built a seven-figure personal income for my family. This decision to "boss up" grew out of a time when I felt something akin to what I feel when flying—a feeling that my life was completely out of control and that I was losing it. I was constantly living in the belief that I was the only one panicking and that I should be ashamed of the fact that I didn't love my role as a stay-at-home mom.

My path to entrepreneurship—or, as I sometimes like to call it, momtrepreneurship—was by no means easy or without mess, but ultimately it has afforded me and my family so many opportunities. My husband and I now own nine businesses, and as a podcaster and author I get to work in my purpose—equipping women, particularly moms, for entrepreneurship.

You guys, there's some stuff in my life that has completely messed me up. I have learned through my thirty-eight years of mess that if I just sit in it and own it, that very mess is usually what leads to success. And y'all, I've seen a lot of mess. That's why I refused to turn down travel last year when this fear of flying started to cause me complete panic attacks. I figure if I can sit through this long enough, eventually it's going to lead to something awesome.**

Right now, though, it feels like our plane is basically a pinball in the sky. I look around to make the "Let's hold hands while we die and pray together" eye contact with anyone on the plane who isn't Michael. But it seems like he and everyone else don't care that soon their lives will be over and our faces will be splashed across CNN for an hour until something more shocking happens. Nobody returns my stare of complete failure to keep it together.

....

* Poor guy. I'm sure he's second-guessed that day he said "I do" while accompanying me on a death flight.

** I'm just not sure what, though, as I sit writing this with sweat dripping down my back, blinking back tears, listening to the captain's voice, which is failing to soothe me in any way whatsoever.

Why is nobody else losing it? I think again. *All right, so I'm doing this one alone. Have it your way, 23C.*

Flying really does put life into perspective, I guess. Nothing helps clarify the essential things in life like near death or the soggy ravioli they serve. That's why I want to share with you my story of wins and lessons and amazingly beautiful stuff, along with the loss and pain and downright ugly stuff that happened along the way to where I am now. I want my story to be the springboard on which you launch your long, successful, amazing career.

I've learned that people who seem to have the most success are those willing to admit they've been through some crap in their lives. I might even venture to say it's the common thread in the people that I watch and find myself wanting to emulate in business. They've got their master's degrees from the school of hard knocks. Learning through the loss and the hurt and the really horrible stuff in life has helped them think in a new way. I dare say it makes them appreciate the hustle. That's not something we should hide. If it creates in us a desire to do better and be more, why aren't we wearing our tragedies and even our failures like a badge of honor? Why are we afraid to show people the chinks in our armor? We all have them.

I'm a dedicated people watcher. Always have been, but I do it for a different reason now. I used to watch others mostly to compare myself with them. *Can I do what she's doing, only better? Does she have something I don't have? What makes him better than me?* Never living up, of course, but you better believe I tried. As I started to mature,* though, I started to see it more as a kind of mentorship—accomplished from afar, without the other person knowing it was happening.

That's not creepy, is it? Maybe it is. But the point is I now watch people to learn from them. And as I've watched, I've noticed that the people who seem to have it all together . . . usually *don't.* Not by a long shot. It's all a show. And chances are that one day those perfect stories will come completely unraveled, that you'll find those perfect people having fights on the Internet and posting long rants on their soon-to-be-radio-silent blogs.

....

* I use that word lightly, friends.

Truth has a way of eventually pouring out. So why not own up to it from the start?

There are only so many hours in the day, and no one can do it all. No mom's kids smile all day while she turns out perfectly shaped pies and ingenious craft projects. Plus, who wants to try to live up to that? Not me. I don't have the freaking time to fill out a perfect planner while I meal plan on the cutest DIY family whiteboard that coordinates with the wall color and to beam over the state of my perfectly organized gift closet.*

This book is my story of entrepreneurship, interwoven with the great lessons I've learned along the way—lessons that anyone with any kind of business can use. I'm not here to say I've learned it all and that what I'm offering here is the path to perfect success. But I've learned a lot and done pretty well for myself, and if I can help you on your path to greatness, well, it's my goal to do so. Actually, it's more than that. It's my joy, my passion, my purpose to do so. I am going to try to be as honest, raw, and real as possible because when women—even bored stay-at-home moms like me—find their purpose, we all win. We need your genius.

As a successful momtrepreneur, I believe in targeting a precise audience for what I'm selling. So I want you to know up front that my target audience is moms like me who dream of running a successful business of their own. Maybe at this point you're like I was five years ago—a stay-at-home mom who wasn't feeling the bliss. Or maybe you're still in the workforce, juggling your job and family responsibilities and wondering if there's a better way. You may be married like I am, or maybe you're a single mom. Possibly you don't even have children yet, but you're looking ahead and trying to figure out how you can build the life you want for your future kids.

If any of these apply, this book is for you. Actually, the philosophies I've acquired in my journey to momtrepreneurship could benefit anyone who is thinking of starting their own business, so you could get something out of this book even if you're an unmarried dude who never plans to have

....

* To be honest, I could probably find the time if it was important, but I'm not that kind of mom, and I'm okay with that.

kids. You'll just have to filter out a few things about motherhood that don't apply to you. The heart of this book is to give you great advice that will help you grow your business, not to be a perfect mom while you do it.

So, friends, are you ready? It's time to buckle up. And it's okay if you feel like you're the only person around you who is losing it. It's okay if you don't know how you're going to pull off the success you have hidden inside of you. It's okay if you've failed in the past. It's all okay. The most important part is that you showed up for this ride in the first place—you're getting on the plane.

Let's be honest. For most people the fear of the journey is enough to squelch their dreams altogether. But not for you. You know as well as I do that there's more out there for you. It's time to boss up and go get it.

1

THE "RIGHT KIND" OF MOM

Have you seen the movie *About Time*? It's one of my favorites. There's a scene in the movie where the aging, sick dad (played by Bill Nighy) is standing in front of his adult son (played by Domhnall Gleeson), and the father gets to choose any time in his life to relive. The moment he chooses reduces me to a puddle of tears because I know it's the scene each and every one of us would choose. The father chooses to go back in time and relive an afternoon at the beach with his adolescent son. They're running around playing, laughing, and not doing anything particularly special except spending time together.

Insert ugly cry.

I don't know about you guys, but to me, being a mother is really hard. It's hard in every way possible—physically, emotionally, mentally, spiritually. But inside all those really hard moments live the most joy and love a human can feel. I can feel totally beat down by motherhood all day and then, five minutes after my kids are asleep, I'll miss them. I live for the vacations away with just my husband, yet about three days in, I wish my three girls were there too. Parenthood is a whirlwind of conflicting emotions, and it's meant to be that way.

The years when my girls were under five were particularly challenging for me. Now that they are ten, ten, and eight, I enjoy being around them a little more, mostly because of the conversations we can now have with them being a little older. Yet there are times when I long for the days when they'd fall asleep on my chest or would hand me fistfuls of weeds picked by the sweetest, chubbiest, little toddler hands. At times I'm tricked into thinking I could have a whole bunch more kids. Then I realize how often I utter the phrase, "This is why we can't have nice things!" and I very quickly change my mind.

Don't get me wrong. After my husband, I love my three daughters more than anything in my life. If given the choice, I'd take a bullet to the head for any one of them. And yet sometimes I don't like being around them. Sometimes they drive me insane. Even as I sit down to write this chapter, I'm sitting on the couch with my three kids running up and down the hall in plastic high heels, playing with remote-control My Little Pony cars that make so much repeated noise I want to scream "I will actually cut you" in my crazy white-lady voice.*

I'm not the picture-perfect mother, and my kids are far from perfect. Want proof? Let me just make you a quick list:

- I've been known to use the iPad as a babysitter.
- My girls sometimes struggle in school.
- One of them is afraid of any weather pattern that doesn't involve cloudless sunshine.
- Another can talk almost anyone into giving her what she wants, and she knows it.
- I'm 100 percent positive that one of them has a hearing problem— despite the fact that we've had her checked—because it is physically impossible for her to listen to my directions the first time around.
- I am not the homeroom mom.
- I take a lot of pride in beating my kids at board games.
- I hate doing laundry and cleaning up after my kids' messes.
- I sometimes yell at my kids when I get frustrated.

....

* You know the one. We all know the one.

- I love Jesus, but sometimes I cuss in front of my kids.*
- I buy sugar cereals and fruit snacks at the store even though I know they're not healthy because, frankly, I value silence.

So, no, I'm not a perfect mom. But I *am* good enough, and good enough is *enough*. You know why? Because I love my kids more than life itself. I'd give up everything for them—even my business if I had to.

The good news, though, is that I don't have to choose, and if you're a mom like me, you don't have to choose either.

You can be both an amazing business owner and a kick-ass mom.

You're Doing It Right

There are a lot of different kinds of mothers. For the intents and purposes of this book, we're going to focus on two different types of moms. The two types cannot be compared, and they are not to be judged for the way they are. They can both be great moms in their own way; they were just designed differently. You may even find yourself hovering between both kinds of moms, and that's okay too. You get to choose the kind of mom and the kind of business owner you want to be.

Bottom line: it's all okay. You're doing it right. Stop worrying. There is no "right kind" of mom.

The first kind of mom is like my sister-in-law, Brittany. This is the woman who likely always wanted to have kids and is deeply fulfilled by doing the good work of being a parent. Her kids came into her life, and they changed her in the best way possible—in the way she's always dreamed. They gave her life purpose, meaning, and weight. And from the time they arrived, she knew that "momming" was her calling in life.

Sure, she sometimes gets frustrated and wishes her kids slept through

....

* To be honest, as long as they use it in the right context, not at someone, and at home, I don't even care if my kids cuss. You can now go to bed knowing you're a better parent than I am. You're welcome.

the night, but overall she revels in the parenting role. She actually enjoys being the homeroom mom. She gets a kick out of taking care of the kids and the house, directing the activities, and keeping everything running smoothly. She takes pride in her contribution to the household. She loves her job as a mom and thrives in her daily schedule with the kids. She revels in watching her kids grow and develop and doesn't want to miss a moment of it.

This kind of woman was made to be a stay-at-home mom. God love her, she was designed for momming. And she's working in the way God created her.

And then there's the second kind of mom—the one who's like me. The kind who was excited to have kids and thought they'd change her. She thought that her life would be given purpose, meaning, and weight once they were placed in her arms at the hospital. That all her dreams and desires would turn with ease toward her kid. That she'd thrive during midnight feedings and science-fair projects.

But it didn't happen.

Instead, she had to admit to herself that she needed more. The dreams and desires she'd had before motherhood hadn't gone away. She loves her kids, but she can't shake the feeling that she was made for something else too. She wants to work in the way God created her, so she seeks out a job or career of some kind. She knows she's a better mother to her kids when she gets a chance to use her gifts and talents in ways that don't specifically relate to her home. God love her, she was made to be a working mom.

If you're reading this book, I'm going to assume it's because you can relate to this second type of mom: you share this desire to work. If you're like me, you're also drawn to the idea of working from home and having your own business, and you want to find a way to make that business profitable.

This does *not* mean you aren't cut out to be a mom. On the contrary, I think moms are often amazing businesswomen, with the capability to do so much to improve the world we live in through their products and their personalities. So what I don't want you to do right now is compare your path to the path of a different type of mom. One thing I know for certain is that some moms want to put all their focus on their home and kids, some want to work outside the home, some want to build businesses of their own—and none of these choices are wrong. All contribute to the family, just in different ways.

Comparing yourself to other moms is discouraging, pointless, and counterproductive. But we do it, don't we? All the time. It's a hard habit to kick.

The Comparison Game

Is there a certain mom you know personally or follow on social media who just seems perfect in every way?

She has one billion followers. Her house is always perfectly curated in that boho, I-didn't-even-try-and-look-how-kitschy-my-house-is style. Her selfies make her look like a goddess at all angles, and she gushes without ceasing over how much she loves being with her kids, who look angelic at all times and probably play silently in their rooms without her ever needing an iPad as babysitter.

How does she do it, guys? She even has time to do her hair and makeup. Does. Not. Compute.

We all have one of these moms in our lives at one point or another. I have one in my social media feed who used to mom at me. She used to decorate at me. She used to take beautiful photos at me. She used to wear size zero jeans at me. She used to have a perfect life at me. Everything she was, did, had, or showed off felt like an attack on my life—until I realized *I* was the only one comparing her life to mine and admitted she was living up to a standard I have no desire or need to uphold.

Surprise—we are different people, and we prioritize different things. She prioritizes making things beautiful because it's what she values. There's nothing wrong with that! But I tend to prioritize authenticity over beauty—often to the point of embarrassment—and real life is what

I document because that is what I value. There's also nothing wrong with that.*

It wasn't her, in other words. It was me. More specifically, it was me and the comparison game I was playing.

PRO TIP

If you find yourself playing the comparison game, here are a few things you can do:

1. Realize *you are the problem here.* That other woman is not comparing her story to yours. She's just telling hers in her way.
2. Remember that nothing and no family is perfect all the time. She's just choosing not to share the mess, and that's okay.
3. The Unfollow button is your friend. If someone (anyone) makes you feel bad about your life on social media, stop following that person!**
4. *Resist the urge to tear the other person down out of your own insecurity.* Don't send that passive-aggressive e-mail or message. Don't write an anonymous hurtful comment. The way we feel about other women says way more about us than it does about them, and lashing out just fuels hurt and misunderstanding.
5. When you find yourself making those comparisons, immediately write down three things that you're grateful for in your own life. Gratitude and comparison don't get along very well.

....

* Just because my kids look like they've been to Fight Club every morning when they wake up and her kids wake ready to be judged by Tyra Banks doesn't mean I'm no good.

** I often wonder if we're torturing ourselves on purpose through our social media feeds.

This is something I have struggled with and will continue to fight against in my own life and business. What is right for you may not be right for someone else, and that really is okay. We can coexist in harmony as different types of moms with different priorities, beliefs, desires, thoughts, actions, and behaviors. But all too often we don't. Somewhere along the line, we decided that the way other people parented was everyone's business and that it was our duty as moms to let others know about it.

Let's Turn the Culture Around

Can I get honest with you? Like super honest?

There are two groups of women I fear more than any other. They're also the two groups I love the most. They're my tribe, my clan, my family, and yet they're the ones I feel judged by the most. They're the ones who tend to be the most cutting when they disagree with me, and they're generally the ones who send the negative e-mails and post the comments that leave me feeling sad.

Who are they?

Moms and Christians.

I say this as both a mom and a Christian, and I've been spending a lot of time turning the finger inward to make sure I am a leader for change in these areas. It's not all of us within these groups, but it's enough to be scary and intimidating—the opposite of who we want to be if we desire to grow as people and as business owners. After all, scary and intimidating is the opposite of the environment that will attract female business owners to the entrepreneurship stage.

I don't know about you, but I don't want to be lumped into a group with people who cut each other down when they disagree. I don't want to have to worry that someone's going to take to the Internet and slam my character if I go out on a limb to speak my own truth. I'm tired of reading social media posts from moms talking about how stupid another mom is for her choices around food, sleep, vaccinations, medicine, school, and so on. Yet that's the mom culture we live in right now.

I hate that someone out there will judge me each time I talk about the way I parent. I hate that our culture covers mothers in shame for their decisions. I hate that we're afraid to show each other the messy side of our parenting for fear we'll be judged for it. Is there no place to just be honest? Is there no place where we have the ultimate right to decide what's best for our kids and then do it without input from others?

I believe there is such a place—but we have to create it. We have to lead.

As moms, let's stop worrying about what's right for other people's kids and focus on our own. Let's give some grace. Let's get off the judgment train and actually support each other. When we see a mom with a kid who is throwing a complete fit because she said no to the candy at the checkout counter, let's give her a fist bump (and a glass of wine if you have one hiding in your purse) instead of the judging eye that says, "My kid would never act like that."* There's enough bad in the world; let's choose the good. More specifically, let's change the culture and love on each other instead of comparing and judging.

Give Up Your Mom Guilt

Because of the current mom culture, for years I stayed silent about wanting something more than just being a mom. I tried on the role of blissfully happy stay-at-home mom and pretended to love it so I'd fit in. I carried a lot of shame about admitting that I had changed my mind about wanting to be a stay-at-home mom.

When you have kids, you completely lose the ability to do one thing at a time, and if you're not careful you can completely lose sight of the person you were before they came along. I found myself on that road. I had choked back all the things I loved because my kids became my sole focus. It all felt so easy, and yet so hard. I thought I was supposed to have it all together, to make things look perfect without so much as a bead of

....

* One way to make sure your kid acts like that is to say they'll never do it, amiright?

sweat and without the lurking feeling that there had to be more. Then came the mom guilt.

Oh mom guilt, how I loathe thee.

It's that sick feeling down deep in your belly that you're doing it all wrong, that you're messing up these tiny, innocent human beings you love with all your heart but sometimes cannot stand to be around. It's hiding your honest feelings—like the fact that you'd rather be working than momming after about five minutes or so with your kids. It's comparing yourself to Jennifer, the homeroom mom, who you just *know* doesn't have these same feelings because she's clearly getting it all right.

I'm convinced this guilt stems from how deeply we love our babies. Nothing brings out so much guilt as the deep desire to do motherhood right. We only get one shot at this, and we have no prior experience. What could go wrong?

Yet there is nothing *right* about this guilt. If we let it, in fact, it can mess up both our lives and our children's lives.

Putting Away the Lawnmower

My own mom was great. We weren't friends when I was growing up because she was my parent. She grounded me, guided me, trained me, and even smacked me in my mouth when I dared sass her—and I don't blame her.* There were times when I was in high school that I thought I hated her, but I was caught up in my teenage angst and guided by my underdeveloped prefrontal cortex, both of which caused me to make terrible decisions. My mom was the truth person I needed in my life but didn't appreciate until my midtwenties. She was always there for me to say the thing I needed to hear, even when I didn't want to hear it. What a gift.

What my mom was *not* always there for was anything and everything I ever needed. She had her own life, responsibilities, and interests that didn't revolve around me or my brothers—and that was okay. There's no way my

* Don't mess with Diane because she will not be having your smart mouth.

mom would tell you she had guilt over working or not being home to jump at my every whim. She'd also tell you that when we were small she did stay home with us, and she took pride in that. At each stage in my childhood, she chose to do what was right for both her and our family, and she saw her responsibility in my life as making sure I grew up able to take care of myself, get a job, and be responsible.

Job done.

My mom was in real estate, and she loved her job. I'm sure she would rather have shown a house than pack me a perfectly balanced lunch with a little note tucked inside. I'm positive she would have wanted to be with a client filling out a contract than at home washing and folding my clothes. So she didn't do the lunch or the laundry. Good thing she didn't have the Internet to make her feel like crap about it. More important, it didn't make her less of a good mom. I'm a better person for the way she parented me, giving me the responsibility of making my own lunch and doing my own laundry. And I have zero residual anger over it.

Let's be honest. Moms now have a different set of standards than our moms did. Did your mom watch you ride your bike out front every second you were out? No, of course she didn't because she was in the house doing stuff and telling you not to come back inside until she called. And yet I feel the pressure to have my eyes on my three daughters every second they're outside, lest something happen and I get called negligent. I can see the comments and hear the rumblings: "Where was her mom? Why wasn't she watching her?" It's what happens every time there's an accident involving a child. Others throw rocks at the mom involved because, of course, she could have prevented this whole thing if she'd just been there.* Come on, ladies.

It's a different world now. The parenting game has changed, and in my opinion the standard has been raised past realistic. I simply do not have the time, energy, or desire to conform in all the ways a mom is supposed to,

....

* How about the dad, Internet? What about the fact that our children make terrible choices (like sticking a fork into an electrical socket for no reason) and that sometimes accidents happen? Oy. Rant over!

and I suspect that's true for most of us. We love our kids, and of course we don't want them to get hurt, but we're being buried under all the responsibility put on us to make sure our kids' lives are free of hard things. We're obsessed with the idea that our kids' struggles are somehow our fault, and we let their struggles reflect on our parenting.

At this point, as a culture, we've completely crushed the helicopter-parenting game, where we hovered over our kids, insulating their lives and making everything safe. We've moved on to "lawnmower parenting,"[1] where parents' lives are consumed with mowing a perfect, struggle-free path for their kids to walk on toward adulthood.

Lawnmower parents spend their time removing every obstacle that could get in the way of their kids' success and happiness, and they feel guilty about every single moment they can't be with their kids, attending to their needs. So they completely replace their own needs, wants, desires, dreams, and goals with their kids' happiness, success, and requirements. They tell themselves that they're sacrificing to make their children's lives better. And yet what they're *actually* producing are entitled, helpless children who have no idea how to solve problems or handle adversity. Cleaning up kids' messes for them simply doesn't prepare them to be responsible adults who know they can do hard things.

The Gift of a Happy Mother

And what about us, ladies? When do we get to make ourselves, our lives, our purposes a priority? After our kids move out of the house?

We love our kids. We do. They're the best things we've ever done. But does that mean everything else we wanted before having children should just float away in a handcrafted papier-mâché hot air balloon that glistens in the sun like a diamond?*

I'm sorry, but enough is enough. I'm tired of the lies we women tell

....

* For all of you who have yet to experience the wonder that is German Glass Glitter, please note that it is the actual devil. You've been warned.

each other in this culture we've created. Doing something you love doesn't make you a bad mom. And guess what? Being there to kiss every boo-boo doesn't make you a good mom.

The way women treat each other over this whole mothering business is shameful and unnecessary. Any guilt you feel over taking time to do something that's fulfilling to you is ultimately self-inflicted and not based on reality. This is where you stop worrying about what people on the Internet say about you, where you stop comparing your real life to somebody else's fake life, and where you start doing what you love because you love it and not because there's pressure to do it.

One thing you can control, which is 100 percent up to you, is giving your children the gift of a happy, fulfilled mother. If that means devoting most of your hours to your home and your kids, fine. But if it means chasing after your dreams while supporting your kids in doing the same, that's fine too. If that means it may shake up the traditional roles in your marriage, do that too. You deserve the same chance at personal fulfillment and happiness as every other member of your family.

About five years ago I finally learned that my life and my purpose do not revolve around my kids. My kids are a blessing, and they certainly fulfill me, but they are not my sole reason for being, and their happiness does not make me worthy of being. I have been given abilities, skills, and gifts that are meant to be used outside of being a mom. And I don't think there's anything wrong with admitting it—or at least I don't think that now.

I don't want to be that woman who has a complete breakdown when my kids leave for college (or whatever they decide to do at age eighteen) because I've attached my worth to my children's lives, their happiness, and their success. I don't want to have to think back about what I liked to do before my kids came along because I can't remember anymore. I don't want to have to try to fall in love with my husband again because we just don't know each other anymore. I certainly don't want to have missed my calling in life because I was too afraid to pursue it while my kids were little for fear of what others would think.

Welcome to Your Turning Point

Does any of this resonate with you? If so, welcome to your turning point. If you're like most women I meet, you're talented, you're a dreamer, you have unique abilities that shine. You could also probably use an extra $500 each month to make ends meet.*

And yes, I've gone from talking about comparisons and guilt and dreams and desires to talking about money. Because let's face it, money matters. It's not everything in life. It's not even the most important thing. But it matters. In fact, that extra five hundred bucks could make a big difference in your life, especially if you're a mom.

I know what you're thinking: *I'd like way more than a car payment each month, but even that would be helpful.* I know because I talk to people just like you who have a dream and a desire to do something more, but who also need just a little bit more money to take some of the pressure off of the household budget.

During the early days of my business, when my paycheck went over $500 a month for the first time, I felt like a weight had lifted from me. Not only was I doing what I loved, but I was contributing financially to my family. My husband and I were on the Dave Ramsey envelope system at that time, and I felt like I had just changed the game.

Earning an extra $500 a month feels like a lot of money, yet it also feels doable. The great news is that you can make that much money at home doing something you love, with your kids at home as well. In fact, you can do a whole lot more than that if you're willing to lean into the mess and figure out how to do it in a way that actually works for you.

The power of that extra $500 is what drives pop-up Etsy shops, online photography studios, eBay resellers, product distributors, and countless other small startup businesses. That $500 moves women to action because women are doers, and they're strong enough to handle motherhood and

....

* There's a lot more where that came from, sister.

their own business at the same time. That $500 is also really fun to chase after. It gives us an excuse* to use our gifts and pursue our purposes, and for stay-at-home moms, especially, it breaks up what can otherwise become a veritable Groundhog Day in our lives.

It's my desire to unlock the potential within each mom to get up and grind out at least that extra bit of income—and maybe lots more. I don't care if it's for the mortgage or shoes; that's up to you. What I care about is that you love making it—because doing something you love is the key.

....
* As if we needed one!

2

THE ROAD MAP TO FREEDOM

I was born to own a business. It's something I have done since I was twenty-three years old, and it's something I'll continue to do for the rest of my life. I come from a long line of entrepreneurial women. As I've mentioned, my mom was in real estate. I worked for her right out of college and learned so much from her about what it takes to run your own business—from setting aside money for taxes to dealing with tough clients. She was brilliant.

My grandma? Also in real estate. One thing she was really proud of was being able to pay for both my mom's and my uncle's college tuition with the money she made as an entrepreneur.

Even my great-grandmother was an entrepreneur. Before it was cool for a woman to run a business, she was doing hair out of her house. My mom used to tell us all the time that my great-grandma would save all of her tip money from doing hair and give it to her when she'd visit.

Clearly, I come by this business-owning dream naturally. I've got a legacy to uphold here, and I will not be one to disappoint. I've learned a lot of hard lessons from the school of hard knocks in my career path, and I've worked in a lot of different fields—from being an Easy-Mac-eating creative freelancer to rising through the ranks of a Fortune 1000 company. At times I've made almost no money working for myself, and other times I've made millions. I've experienced wild amounts of freedom and crushing loss. All those experiences make me the momtrepreneur I am today and fill me with a desire to use my story to help other women achieve success in business as well.

When I was able to find something to do that encompassed all the lessons I'd learned and the skills I possessed, my business took off like lightning out of the sky, and it's still going strong. The best part about finally finding my "thing" has been the flow that followed. I've been able to experience freedom at work just as I do in my life outside of work.

That doesn't mean that everything I do is fun and that everything's perfect. But it does mean that when I sit down to do my job, I am confident in myself and my work, and more days than not, the eight hours I've worked feel more like three.

Before I let you in on the success philosophies that my business was built on, I want to tell you more of my story. I want you to see that while the details may not be the same, we're more alike than different. So let's get to know a little bit about a younger Lindsay.

The Younger Me

At eight years old I used to tell people I wanted to be an astronaut when I grew up. I didn't really want to be an astronaut though. That just seemed like the normal thing kids my age would say. I actually wanted to be the boss of a business. As crazy as that sounds for an eight-year-old, this is truly what I wanted.

I remember one day walking through the Safeway in Ahwatukee, Arizona, with my mom. I usually went with her when she hit the grocery store. Sometimes she'd let me take the back roads and drive us to the store before I had a license. She was that kind of mom.* Almost every time we went to the store, she'd grab a loaf of French bread fresh from the bakery (hot if we were lucky), and we'd eat it as we walked around

....

* I can't get arrested for admitting to breaking the law twenty-five years after the fact, can I?

the store shopping. Super healthy, I know, but what a great memory with my mama!

On that particular day when we were walking through the Safeway, I was thinking very hard about what I was going to be when I grew up. I knew I was different from the other girls in my class, and I also knew that I couldn't wait until the day I was free to make my own choices and live away from home. The other girls in my class wanted to be ballerinas and doctors and princesses. But I wanted to be an entrepreneur. And I wanted to provide a product that everybody needed because, if everybody needed it, I could maximize profits.*

This ambition came partly from the fact that entrepreneurship was truly a part of my DNA, but it also grew out of the reality that we didn't have a lot of money. I always knew that I would have to make money to buy the things I wanted to have and do. I also knew that my parents weren't living that kind of life. I felt our financial struggles at an early age.** And I just figured that finding something everyone needed was the best way to make money on a product.

As I walked through the store, scanning the shelves for the products that could perhaps fit into my "everybody needs this" category, we happened to turn down the paper goods aisle.

That's it! I thought. *Everybody needs toilet paper.****

My elementary school brain led me to believe that one person owned each company that produced toilet paper and that I would be one of them one day. I just knew I was going to figure out a way to disrupt the toilet paper game. You guys. Bless my heart. I wish this was a lie.

As I grew, I got a better sense of how the toilet paper game really went,

....

* If you haven't figured this out yet, I was never popular or cool—because, sadly, "maximize profits" is not a goal that wins friends and influences people in elementary school.

** Which is also what led me to having real conversations about money with my kids this year. Kids know if their families are struggling. It was the right choice for us to talk with them about money even if we aren't riding the struggle bus right now.

*** I would be remiss if I didn't also mention that for about a year when I was twelve, I thought I could strike it rich if I owned a company that produced socks that you could use on your hands or feet. Face palm.

and I also realized that producing butt-wiping tools wasn't for me. Don't get me wrong; toilet paper is good to have. It's just not my life calling, but it put me on the right track. Even though my business ideas changed as I matured, that desire to own my own business and make money with it remained an integral part of me.

Knowing what she did about entrepreneurship and the difficulties that come along with it, my mom convinced me to get a degree in business and communication. That wasn't really a request, but more of a requirement.* She almost convinced me to go into pharmaceutical sales after college at Arizona State** because, to her, that was a safe job that would provide a great salary, advancement opportunity, and challenge without all the risk that comes along with business ownership. The problem with that was I had no desire to drive around Arizona in the summer, when the temps reach 374 degrees,*** and schlep medical equipment all over the place. So I made a case for going to work for my mom in her office. That way I could earn a paycheck while I figured out what I really wanted to do.

During that time, I picked up photography and some design skills. I used them to help my mom market the homes she listed and help her clients get a better picture of what she could do for them. I started creating marketing pieces for other agents in my mom's office as well—my very first side hustle, at age twenty-three. Then one day I happened to walk into a scrapbook store, and my whole world changed.

Scrapbooking was the hobby that brought together all of the things I was good at and loved to do. I loved to use my hands and my computer to make pretty things full of color, and I loved to write out my stories. So I got into scrapbooking big-time. And my very first business—the kind where you form a Limited Liability Company and make it legit— was a freelance scrapbooking and photography business. Now, I know what you're thinking: *But Lindsay, all the coolest twenty-five-year-olds are scrapbooking on the weekends. How did you pull that off with so much*

....

* And as the oldest child, I assumed it was my duty to be responsible and do what Mom said. I am in all ways the typical oldest child.
** Go, Devils!
*** That's science.

competition? (Commence eye roll.) Well, I'm here to tell you, again, that I'm not cool by normal standards. I like weird things.

Eventually I left the comfort of my mom's office and took hourly jobs at a few scrapbook stores in Arizona because I just fell in love with the industry so much, I could no longer think about the real-estate market. Despite my mom's not-so-subtle urging, real estate just wasn't what I loved. I knew it wasn't the career path for me. Scrapbooking was what I loved.* So I spent my days working at scrapbook stores and my nights creating projects for magazines and product manufacturers to help them sell their product.

I was just learning how to run a business, of course, so I made a lot of mistakes. The number-one mistake I made in my first freelance business was not making any money. Try to contain your shock and awe. It's not enough to just want to love what you do and have a product that works. The other part of that formula involves getting paid for your work. You need to make money doing what you're doing so that you can, you know, pay your bills. My early failures, though, were necessary lessons to prepare me for my future business-ownership opportunities.

I failed to think through the part of the business-building formula that required me to bring in a profit. I had plenty of people who would pay me. They just paid me next to nothing because I wasn't valuing my time or understanding the market and charging accordingly. I was having a great time, I was young, and I ate boxed macaroni and cheese like it was a gourmet meal. What did I care about making tons of money? I was having too much fun. And I wasn't entirely sure that having fun and making money could coexist.

Eventually, though, my mom sat me down and got real with me. She reminded me what she had already taught me through her example—that it's important to be compensated for your time, no matter how much you like what you do. I realized she was right. If I wanted to actually make being an entrepreneur work, I would have to bring in enough money to survive on it.**

....

* Still do because I'm just as cool fifteen years later.
** Also, I was growing sick of powdered cheese, even though it *is* the best, and I

It was time to let the full-time freelancing go and get a "real job" that would pay me a salary, make good use of my education, and even provide health benefits. (I was sure I'd come back to freelancing once I had a full-time job to support my scrapbooking habit.) A friend of mine who had recently made the jump from an hourly to a salaried position had just the hookup for me. So I joined a Fortune 1000 company, and over the next six years I worked my way up from the bottom to management evaluation and training.

This is where I got my first glimpse at leadership in a corporate setting. My team was responsible for hitting required sales and retention benchmarks, and we competed against the other teams of salespeople on the floor. It was at this company that I realized I have a gift for sales. I naturally understood how to get people to say yes to me, and I could present the value of our product in a way that made the customer feel good about their choice. That's probably why mom had pushed me into medical sales and real estate. The apple doesn't fall far from the tree, as they say.

When I was promoted into management, I was one of only two female managers. When the senior director gave me the position, he stood in front of me while I sat on a chair in front of him and said, "You're not going to make me regret hiring you, are you?" I could physically feel how much he wished I was a man. At that time the standard hire for the position was a man, and the boys club at that organization was firmly in control. Hiring me was shaking things up. And even though I was fully qualified, I knew he was nervous to promote a woman over another dude.* I was learning through experience just how real that glass ceiling is.

The minute I heard those words, I knew I'd ultimately have to find my way back to entrepreneurship—where I would be able to make my own rules, my own hours, and not worry about some dude I don't know being disappointed by my performance before I even start.** Entrepreneurship was calling me.

....

have even been known to steal bites from my kids in recent days.
* But I had crushed my interview, and I knew he was under some pressure to pick me despite the fact that I have a vagina.
** Insert biggest eye roll imaginable.

For the record, though, my team of all women (except two brave men) eventually wiped the floor with the other teams. Women are awesome. We can do whatever is asked of us, even under all the pressure and all the stereotypes. How's that for making the guy regret hiring me?

I held on to the scrapbooking business for a little while after going to work at the company, but eventually I had to let it go because it was a terrible business plan for me. But I never let photography go. Even with my nine-to-five job, photography held strong.[*] I started taking weekend family photography gigs, and I started charging what my work was worth, even to my friends and family. I got plenty of inquirers who wanted to trade me my services for "experience or exposure," which I learned very quickly would not be accepted as a form of payment for my cell-phone bill.[**]

PRO TIP

Pay for services and products from those who provide them to you. Don't put your friends in a weird spot of saying they'll take your family pictures or give you that face treatment for free just because you know them. You should pay for their hard work *because* you know them and you want to support them.

On the other side of that coin, charge people for the products and services you provide. Your time and your product are not free. Require payment even if you're doing work for people you know and love. This is what you do. If you want to justify your time working, you need real dollars.

....

[*] It still does. The skill has served me well, and I still use it in every business I own to this day.
[**] Just try letting AT&T know you're sending them a voucher for the exposure you got next month. Stop the insanity!

The Moment Everything Changed

During those six years when I was working in corporate America, I met my husband (at an ASU game*), got married, gave birth to a set of identical twin girls, and then, not even two years later, to another baby girl.

My family life was lit, y'all. That's when the biggest change in my life happened.

Three weeks after Kennedy, my youngest, was born, my husband pulled me into our living room and sat me down on the couch. He looked at me with more pity than I had ever experienced—that is *not* a good feeling—and said to me, "Lindsay, I have to tell you something, and it's going to be the hardest thing you've ever heard."

Never once had what he was about to say ever crossed my mind.

He looked at me with tear-filled eyes. "Your mom died today."

Lights. Out.

Everything has been different from this moment on in my life. Everything.

I threw whatever it was I'd been nervously playing with in my hands onto the coffee table, put my hands over my face, and screamed. Michael sat motionless across from me, trying like hell to keep himself together.

I remember asking, "What? How? What happened?" My mind went to a car accident—of course it did. Just three weeks earlier, Mom had been at my house with me while we brought her third granddaughter into the world. She had seemed perfectly healthy. She was only fifty-three.

But it hadn't been a car accident. She'd been at home.

I made too many difficult phone calls to count, the saddest of them to my two younger brothers. I wondered how we were going to get two one-year-olds and a newborn to Arizona for a funeral when I was still recovering from my C-section. *We don't even have enough laps for them to sit on.* And also: *I can't do this. I still look pregnant!* **

....

* Go, Devils—again!

** I am totally that vain, I'm sorry to say. My mother dies, and I'm worried about showing my gut in front of the thousands of people I know will show up for her funeral. Then again, grief does crazy things to your mind.

I remember snapping right into work mode though. Efficient as ever. *Okay, I can handle this. I'll figure it all out and fix it. Right now I need to feed the baby. We should eat our dinner. We need to get the groceries . . .*

My brain was half shut off, and I was in complete and total shock. I could feel without feeling. I would start to cry during the night, but for some reason I couldn't get myself to believe it was true. I had to have logical conversations with myself. *Lindsay, no, you can't call her to tell her what's going on. She isn't there. You already know this.*

I couldn't tell which end was up, really. I just walked around in a fog. I retained my ability to do the things I had to do for the family to survive, but I wasn't in my right mind.

It wasn't until I walked into the room for the private viewing and saw my mom lying on a table that it started to become real. For some strange reason I was shocked to see her there. Though I knew why we were there, somehow I didn't expect to see her. I can't explain that feeling. But I knew in that moment that she was really gone. There was no part of her lying on that table, save for a few recognizable physical traits I had known all my life. I remember her hands. I had to see her hands.

It turns out that my healthy, worked-out-every-day mom had died of a massive heart attack due to the buildup of scar tissue in her heart from a previous heart attack she didn't even know about. She hadn't recognized what was happening when she had her first heart attack. She thought she had the flu. I remember everything about that day. She was probably the exact age that I am right now, maybe a year or two younger, and I was in junior high. One morning she called me quietly from her bathroom and she told me she couldn't move. She asked me to go get her some medicine from the convenience store, and I rode my bike down there to get it.

She was under massive amounts of stress at that time: financial, emotional, relational; her role as a mother, her marriage, her work—massive pressure. She held it all together, though, as efficient and unfeeling as ever. *I can handle this. I'll figure it all out and fix it.* Sound familiar?

Nothing can convince me that stress didn't kill my mom. That is one piece of history I cannot let repeat itself.

There was a time after losing my mom when I thought that if I kept pushing through, I might get back to my old normal. I realize now that I won't. Everything is still different. I cry less each year, but there's still a big hole in my soul where only a mom can go, and I know now it will always be there.

Good things still happen, of course. But victory is just a little less sweet. At holidays there's just a little less laughter. During the girls' events there's a little less excitement. They don't know it, but I do.

I think that's also where my fear of flying stems from—from the possibility that I may eventually bestow this kind of loss on my kids, that they may have to experience this kind of hole in their own heart one day. For some reason my brain has calculated that a plane crash is the most likely scenario in which I might not live to see my girls grow up. I realize that's totally illogical when you say it out loud, but it all boils down to grief.

Losing my mom is by far the hardest thing I've walked through, and my childhood wasn't a cakewalk. I continue to walk through it. It feels like wading through thick molasses. Nothing about it feels good although I can acknowledge some good that came out of it, important lessons I learned that have helped me.

For example, sometimes I wonder what I would be doing if my mom were still here, and each time I land on the fact that I probably wouldn't have the capacity to do what I'm doing today. It's through and because of the broken parts of me that I've come to believe that almost anything is possible. Not because my mom didn't teach me this with her words or by her example—because she did—but because I didn't know for sure that I could do it until she wasn't there to catch me if I didn't. Amazing things happen when you realize you have no safety net. That's the hardest and best lesson I've learned so far in my life.

Another lesson I learned through my mom's death was one that put me on the path I'm on right now. When she died, she was in debt, she worked crazy hours, she had a lot of dreams and plans to travel the world and see her grandkids grow up. My mother regularly told me she was going to live to be one hundred, and she also regularly told me about all the things she was going to do someday. "Someday I'm going to go to Italy and drink the wine in Tuscany. Someday I'm going to take us on a river rafting trip down the Colorado River in the Grand Canyon. Someday . . ."

She died with all of her somedays still sitting on the table, waiting to be realized.

Look, I know my mother's death came at the right time. I believe her days and hours and breaths were numbered and it was the right time for her to go. I realize she's a whole lot happier in heaven, even having never seen Italy.

But here on earth? Her story is hard for me to tell. I feel a certain amount of guilt around how hard she worked to provide for my brothers and me and how little she got to do for herself. There was no happy ending for her in life, just a lot of struggle to survive. She never made it to that place in this life where she got to relax and experience freedom.

Having seen that, as much as I admired my mom, I'm determined that her story will not be my story. I will not let my kids feel about my life the way I feel about my mom's life. If I die at fifty-three, as she did, I want them to stand at my funeral and say, "She may have only lived fifty-three years, but she did a hundred years' worth of living."

A Plan in Motion

In the months after my mother died, it became clear to me that something had to change. There I was with a newborn and a pair of one-year-old twins. I was working full time at a Fortune 1000 company and a little over halfway through my master's degree in Organizational Psychology. We were in Colorado at that time, and I didn't have any of the comforts of home in Arizona, where I was raised. It was just too much. So I started grief counseling and somehow managed to resist the urge to stay in bed and sleep through part of my life because I had babies that needed me.*

....

* What a gift, truly. As hard as I've found motherhood to be, my children saved me through the hardest part of my life so far.

And after talking a lot with my husband, I set a plan in motion to earn the freedom to actually live my life.

I would quit my corporate job, finish my degree, and stay home with the girls while building my own photography business. Meanwhile, Michael would concentrate on building his career. He and I had agreed before we even had children that we'd move as much as we needed to for his career to take off. And move we did—every single year for the first nine years of our marriage.

We struggled financially as I started and restarted my photography business in all the cities we moved to. But I was determined not to go back to a corporate job, and my husband supported me every time I had to start over.

By 2013, just over two years after my mom died, we had moved to Seattle, Washington, where my husband had climbed the corporate ladder to his dream job—college president. He was bringing his best to work every day and working crazy hours. Twice when we had a vacation planned, his boss made him call me at the eleventh hour and cancel because she wanted him at work. He was giving all of his energy and empathy at work, and when he'd get home, he was tapped out. He had nothing left to give. How could he after a twelve-hour workday? How could he with only one day off a week?

Stress was going to kill him, too, and I felt certain that I needed to find us a new normal, a new way to do life. Losing one family member to stress-related illness was enough to light a very real fire under my butt to find a solution to the problem.

It was in Seattle that I tried an essential oil for the first time, and it was there that I put together the business plan that was going to change my life and the life of my family. This was going to be the thing that took the stress off Michael. This was going to be the thing that would provide the money for a Christian education for my kids. This was going to be the way God allowed me to provide a different kind of legacy for my kids—to break the cycle of stress and change our family heritage.

People often ask if I knew when I started my oils business that it was going to take off, and my answer is unequivocally *yes*. I knew it as surely as I knew my own name. This was going to be the vehicle that got us the freedom to say yes to opportunity, to live a different kind of life.

I'm not the one who typically hears the still, small voice of God. I talk too much. I do too much. I don't take enough time to sit down and allow myself to be quiet. But after a couple of months trying to push away the idea of trying out an essential oil business, I woke up with a fully formed idea for marketing them in a new way. It was like I had been given the clearest vision for what I was supposed to do. I got up out of my bed in the middle of the night and pounded out my plan on a computer. I just knew I was supposed to follow this calling—and that certainty, my friends, was a God thing. My steps were directed that night, not in a still, small way but in a loud, booming voice, through a desire I could not shake.

I knew I was supposed to walk through the door of this essential oils business when I realized I could use my authentic voice, my skills, and my talents toward something I was super passionate about—women's entrepreneurship. I love the product we sell, and it does so much good for so many people, including my family. But I don't love any product in the world the way I love teaching women how to build a successful business. That, my friends, is my passion.

On March 25, 2013, the Lemon Droppers—my team of essential oil freaks—was born. My focus from day one was to teach these women how to work smart, be themselves, and build a business that could bring them the freedom to choose the kind of life they wanted to live.

But before that happened, I had to come to terms with the fact that I was getting myself involved with a type of company that I deeply distrusted—to put it mildly.

The First Big Score

Multilevel Marketing (MLM), direct sales, and network marketing had always been like cuss words to me, and honestly some of the MLM industry still is.* When I hear them or say them, I immediately feel like I've been punched in the stomach. It is shocking how many negative connotations

....

* There are some words that I hate worse ("*moist*," anyone?), but not many.

those phrases carry with them in my mind. Everything I had heard about and experienced around how MLM sells and markets their product had struck me as sleazy and manipulative. And I just knew the same thing was going through the heads of my tribe, my generation, my friends, and my sphere of influence.

So when I found out that the essential oils company I was interested in was an MLM—I swear I didn't know at first!—I was beyond furious. *Oh, great*, I thought, *we're about to get into the weird that inevitably follows every person I have ever known to be involved in direct sales.**

The problem was, by that point, I'd already fallen in love with essential oils. I became obsessed not about doing the business but about using the product. And as I do with all things I love, I talked about them on my social media feed.

At the time I only had about two hundred fifty followers, and it was really just made up of photo/scrapbook people, friends, and family. Nothing to write home about, but enough to launch a business that would eventually lead to really big things. Once I started posting about the product and started talking honestly about what I loved, I found myself answering a lot more questions about how to get oils than talking about ballet practice and what I ate for lunch. And I loved every second of it.

Gone were the days when my Facebook and Instagram and Twitter feeds were filled with every nuance of my day. Instead, I was finding ways to connect and to market the product I had decided to sell as a business.

The fact that I was a complete network-marketing virgin actually turned out to be an advantage. I didn't know anything about it. So I searched everywhere for information on how people were growing a business like this. I also watched what my competition was doing. How were they working? What did they do to attract customers? How did they communicate? What need were they meeting for their customers? Then I went out and did the exact opposite. And you know what? It worked.

I'd seen enough of what the typical MLM salesperson did to make money and, honestly, I didn't like it that much. I noticed most leaders I

....

* Again, I'm weird—but not *that* kind of weird.

studied in the industry were inauthentic and generally pretty entitled, as a whole. I noticed that the culture of many MLM businesses seemed sneaky and self-serving. I always felt like the salesperson's paycheck, not the value of the product for the customer, was the point of every transaction. In my opinion, that wasn't right. I once had a network marketing distributor tell me that if I really wanted to find $2,000 to buy their product, I could make it happen even though he knew Michael and I were struggling financially at that time.

I wanted to create a business from home that was consistent with my personal values and that allowed me to actually meet the needs of my customers while making money at the same time. I'm not in the business of making my friends and family take my awkward phone call where I explain the "opportunity" I have for them or where I beg them to buy product every month so I can build my paycheck. I'm most certainly not in the habit of making people tell me no nine times before I leave them alone.

So I decided to try out MLM my way, a totally different way. We're talking *wildly* different. Black and white, Sylvester and Tweety, oil and water—you get the point. Opposite. This was something I was not willing to compromise on. I was going to be myself, and I was going to sell my product in a way that ran counter to what I saw happening with every other MLM.

And guess what? So far, not only have I seen amazing success based on this model, but it's been in record-setting time. In five years, the team that started with me and an Instagram post has grown to more than 520,000 families and a third of a billion dollars in annual sales. Within a year and a half of starting, I was pulling in more than six figures a month in personal income.

I quickly realized that those six figures were buying me freedom. I could say yes to life, to fun, to travel, to giving, and I could say yes to other business opportunities. Since my first million-dollar-producing business, my husband and I have created two businesses (on the retail and services side of entrepreneurship) that have gone on to produce more than a million dollars each. Without the success of that first venture, I would have had no ability to take the lessons I'd learned and apply them to something new.

I'm still not your typical MLM person. I love the company I represent, and I love my team and our products, but I still cringe about the pressure many network marketing reps put on the people they know to buy product to build a paycheck. I wish they could see there's a better way to reach customers, one that works the same for any and all entrepreneurs, no matter what industry they're in, what product they represent, or what service they provide. The best way I've found to make that kind of change in an industry has been to teach the women I work with and speak to that entrepreneurship doesn't have to mean desperation and garages full of product they can never sell.

Your Purpose or Your Vehicle

Over the years of getting to know the MLM industry, I've realized that it can be a great source of residual income. But it can also be a great vehicle for getting women to the place where they can fulfill their purpose in life. That's what it was for me.

The same is true of any kind of entrepreneurship. Maybe your product is your purpose. Maybe your service is your purpose. That's okay. Maybe those extra five hundred bucks are your purpose, and that's okay too.

Maybe, though, your product or service is actually the vehicle that gets you to your real purpose.

I had to build my business success first before I was able to step out and lead female entrepreneurs in any industry the way I do today. I had to have the money to build a speaking career. I had to realize a certain amount of success before I had the ability to write books on how to achieve it.

You get to choose. Your business is either your purpose or your vehicle. Both are okay. Either way, you're doing it right.

When people ask me about my success secrets, I tell them about the ten success philosophies that I and so many others have used to build our businesses. It doesn't matter what business or industry you're in or what level of success you've reached; these ten philosophies can apply to your business too. They are foundational tools. You learn the foundation and then, in your own way, with your own voice, you go out and make them work for your business. I've applied them to nine different businesses I've owned in the last five years—always in a different way because each business requires different kinds of work.

As we explore the ten success philosophies, you won't find me saying you have to do anything a certain way. We are all different, and we all work best when we use our unique talents and skills to build our businesses. This book isn't about you building your business my way. On the contrary, it's about you taking these foundations and making them work for you.

It's likely that you grabbed this book because you're either currently running a business that you'd like to see grow or you've got a little idea that you haven't quite gotten off the ground yet. Both are awesome, and you've come to the right place.

Before we move on to the ten success philosophies, I want you to take a good look at who you are, what you're good at, and what you really want out of life—because it's really hard to get where you're going if you don't know where you're coming from.

But what if you don't know? What if you're not sure what you're good at anymore (besides changing diapers)? What if you've lost touch with what inspires you and calls to you and you can't even remember all the things you used to love and all the things you're good at?

Don't worry girl, I got you. I'm positive that your skills and passions will help you turn your desire to own your own business into a reality.

Read on.

3

FINDING YOUR THING

Do you even remember what your life was like before you had kids?
Remember getting all stressed out about something you thought was really complicated—before children came along and compounded the complication factor of literally everything you do?

Ever found yourself trying to breathe more quietly while tiptoeing out of a room with a sleeping kid?

I rest my case.

Maybe you were a total a-hole about child-raising, like I was before I became a mom. Y'all, I was the queen of the jerks. I was absolutely sure I would be the exception to the walking horror film that is motherhood for the average woman. I was going to nail momming in a way no mom had mommed before. I'm talking losing the baby weight, keeping the monthly girls' nights, being strict but loving, avoiding the grocery store meltdowns, and making dinners every member of the family would eat without so much as a whimper. In fact, my kids would eat broccoli for dessert.

Oh, ignorant bliss.

Then motherhood came upon me like a freight train, and I failed at living for basically three entire years of my life. And I don't say "failed at living" in a way that snotty moms say it as they serve you freshly baked cookies and pretend it's their bad day (cue neck punch). I mean I barely functioned enough to keep my kids alive. Plus, my boobs now point in the wrong direction, and I wear Spanx like a NASCAR driver wears a sponsor sticker.

I don't even look the same after those first three years, let alone think the same. And yet that person I used to be before I became a mom is still in there somewhere.

That's true for you, too, even though you may have forgotten. So take a minute to think about what you were like before kids. What did *you* like to do? What were you good at? Did you have hobbies? What did you love to talk about?

Can we just stop to notice that in approximately zero of the mental lists of answers to the above questions did someone include "taking actual notes about my kids' dumps"? Our lives have changed since having kids, and our priorities have changed too. But does that mean we're completely different people who magically woke up and cared how many days had passed without our kids taking a successful nap?

No. No, it does not. We care about our kids, and so we do the things moms need to do and a lot of the stuff we think moms are supposed to do. But be honest—wouldn't you rather binge an entire season of the latest adult series on Netflix than watch a single episode of *Caillou* . . . again?*

Sometimes I wonder what I cared about so much before kids. How did I fill up my days? What did I really have to juggle? What did I really love? I can't always remember and, you know, I choose to believe that's kind of normal. After all, for most of us, our kids took away our ability to cough without peeing our pants, so why wouldn't they take our memory too? (It just keeps getting more glamorous, amiright?)

It may be time to start walking through a few doors and trying on the possibilities of what we like again. Maybe we can set aside some time to admit there may be life outside of our children and maybe we should be a part of it. Let's finally let our brains process the fact that we don't have to be in love with every second of motherhood and find it the most exhilarating experience of our lives. Feeling that way doesn't mean we don't love our

....

* Because Caillou is the devil.

kids or that we aren't good moms. It means we're getting real about what's calling us—and doing our best to listen.

Let me be quite honest with you. About nineteen days into my rookie year of motherhood, when my second twin came home from the NICU, I realized momming wasn't going to be the thing that fulfilled me. I'm pretty sure I realized it at two in the morning as I tried to balance two babies on an impossibly small pillow to feed them while at the same time having a massive fight with Michael over who was the most tired. It was in that moment that a horrible wave of shame came over me as I thought to myself, "I actually hate this."

And yes, things did get better as time went on. I didn't hate momming all the time. Sometimes I even loved it. But I wanted something more too. I wanted something that was just mine.

I struggled for years with my conflicted feelings though I told approximately zero people about them. How could I admit these things to anyone?

Time went by, but my desire to be labeled as more than just a mother didn't go away. I still wanted something that was my own. Something that used the brain God had given only to me and the skills and talents I had developed over my years before kids. I worked hard on developing those skills and talents. And so did you, remember?

No?

Well, let me help you remember.

In this chapter we're going to explore a few options for finding your "thing"—that combination of nonparenting-related interests, skills, and desires that could be transformed into your successful business.

The You Before Diapers

I find that moms are almost afraid to dwell on their dreams and desires and non-kid-related interests because they think they're not allowed to do that anymore. *It's wrong. It would screw up the works. What would the husband say? What will the Internet think?*

This is where I need you to remember that you aren't worried about what anyone else thinks. And after that, you need to jog your memory about what life was like for you before the kids arrived. Below are a few questions for you to answer about your past life. I highly suggest you ask your spouse or your besties for help with many of them because bad memory postmotherhood is for reals, y'all.

What was your favorite way to spend an afternoon?

_____

What was your favorite job?

_____

What were some of your favorite hobbies or pastimes?

_____

What were you good at doing (skills, talents, and so on)?

_____

How did you fill your time once you were home from school or work?

_____

What could you not wait to do after school or work?

_____

What kinds of ideas would you fill notebooks, journals, or sketchbooks with?

_____

What did you like to make?

_____

What kinds of activities were you excited to plan?

_____

What did you daydream about?

_____

What did you assume you'd do in the future?

_____

What did you want to do or be?

_____

What did you teach other people?

_____

If you're married, what was it that you and your spouse first connected over?

_____

What is one of the greatest compliments you've ever gotten about something you made or did?

_____

Is that picture of the you before babies becoming a bit clearer?

But don't stop there. It's important to recover the forgotten you, but you also want to think forward to what is calling you *now*. It might well be an old dream, but it might be a new one too, something that has recently awakened in your heart and soul and mind. Maybe something you have discovered about yourself.

What can you not stop thinking about? What do you find yourself doing when you procrastinate? What sneaks into your mind during your "breaks" from momming?*

....

* Oh, are we calling locking-ourselves-in-the-closet-to-eat-chocolate-again a break? How about when your kids are putting their faces up to the crack under the door to your toilet to talk to you while you do your business? These are *not* breaks. But if you ever get a minute to yourself (Naptime? An afternoon when a babysitter is over?), take some time to think through these questions.

That is likely the thing you should be trying to create a business around.

I'm not talking about skills at this point. Skills you can learn with a search of the Google machine and maybe a little practice. Or skills you already have can be repurposed to serve a new endeavor. They're important, but they're also secondary.

The question you really need to answer at this point is *What do you love?* What fills you up? What makes you feel like you? What sort of things get you excited and make you feel alive?

I really want you to nail this down before you move on to identifying your gifts, talents, abilities, and skills. And you can do it, I promise. You cared deeply about something once—and it's time you found that girl again.

It's time to reconnect with your passion.

What's Your Passion?

When it comes to starting a business, it's so important to pinpoint what you're passionate about doing so you can incorporate your true passions into what you do. If you have no passion in your work, it will be the first thing you toss out the window when the going gets hard—and I promise you, it's going to get hard. You must love what you're doing and what you're working for. You must have your heart in the game. It's what will get you through a lot of the tough days because you will always be able to find something that builds you up in the midst of everything that pulls you down.

I would be remiss if I didn't talk about the difference between a passion and a hobby. I'm about to drop a couple of dictionary definitions on you so we can get the precise difference (I know, I know . . . get excited!).

The definition of passion is: "a strong liking or desire for or devotion to some activity, object, or concept." A hobby, however, is "a pursuit outside one's regular occupation, engaged in especially for relaxation."

The key difference here is that one is an activity you do to relax. That's a hobby. But the other is something you do because you absolutely love it, something that draws you strongly and inspires a strong devotion in you. That's a passion.

Now, it's possible to turn your hobby into a business. (It's also possible for a hobby to grow into a passion.) But you're much more likely to flip your passion into a business because of the single word that differentiates these definitions: *devotion*. Something you're devoted to isn't something you can put aside for a time without really missing it. It's something that calls to you, that energizes you, that you can't ignore. That's what you should spend the hours of your life doing.

Here are some questions that may help spark ideas about what you are passionate about. For these questions, I want you to try to find different answers for each one of them, to give yourself some options. Many of these questions will make you think long and hard about yourself, which can be difficult. Introspection isn't always easy, but it is necessary. So take some time to fill out the answers—and do it on the basis of you and you alone. A lot of us moms tend to answer questions like these with our kids in mind. We respond as caregivers rather than independent women. So try to withhold judgment and not worry about what you think you should say or what your family would want you to say.

If you had no choice but to enter the next TV talent show, what would you choose to do?

_____

What type of problem would your friends or family most likely call you to help them with?

_____

When you were little, what did you dream about?

_____

What kind of how-to segment could you teach on your local news channel?

_____

What magazine articles or books do you find yourself reading?

_____

If you were charged with making a do-it-yourself gift for a friend, what would you make?

_____

If you had two weeks of free time away from your daily grind, what would you spend the time doing?

_____

What is one thing you find yourself talking about over and over?

_____

What do you enjoy that most people would be surprised to learn?

_____

What is one thing you do that produces the feeling of joy inside you (I often call these butterflies)?

_____

What's one thing you haven't done a lot but you loved when you tried it?

_____

If you were to write a book, what could you write about?

_____

Once you answer the questions honestly, put a little mark next to each of the passions you like the most. If you get stuck, imagine that tomorrow is the last day of your life and you can do only one thing from your list. What would you choose? Do that over and over again until you come up with your top five passions, and list them below.

1. _____

2. _____

3. _____

4. _____

5. _____

Skills, Talents, and Abilities

Do you have a better idea by now about what you like and care about? When I answer these questions, I feel a little more connected to the chick I was before I had kids. That's the important first step in discovering what kind of business you should look into. The second step is to identify the things you're naturally good at or the skills you've developed in the course of your lifetime.

Can you imagine a career where you can actually combine the things you're passionate about with the things you're really good at to make buckets of money? Is that not the dream? Imagine what it would feel like to be filled up by what you get to do and then find someone has put money in your bank account for doing something you'd have likely done for free? That's the beauty of combining your passions with your skills. So let's dig a little deeper to locate some of the places your abilities coincide with your passions. That intersection is where you'll find the right business for you.

Skills can be a double-edged sword. I find there are quite a few things I'm skilled at that I have absolutely no desire to do. For example, I'm pretty good at hooking up electronics and figuring out which wires go where and turn on what components. It's something I really have a knack for. Doing that task, however, makes me want to scoop my eyeballs out with spoons.

I hate doing it. The fact that I *can* do it doesn't mean I *like* doing it or that I should do it.

You're probably going to discover something similar as you learn about your skills. There will likely be a few things you're good at but hate doing—that you'd rather run a marathon barefoot on a path of Legos than do. There will probably be others that you can do well but simply don't care about.

That's okay. I get you. Don't worry, we're going to make sure to separate the list of skills into *yes* and *no* and *maybe* piles.

Step 1: Grab yourself a black pen and a red pen.

Step 2: Come up with a list of three life wins and list them in the spaces below. A win is a situation where you feel you came out on top, where you achieved something. To help you get a wide range of answers, choose one win from your childhood (under 18), one as a young adult (in your twenties or early thirties), and one that occurred in the last five years.

WIN 3: _____

WIN 2: _____

WIN 1: _____

Step 3: Notice that there are three columns of the same skill. This is so you can do this exercise for each of your wins. In this step you'll go through the list of skills with a black pen and circle every skill you were required to use during your wins.

For example, if my win was that I successfully mediated a disagreement between coworkers, I would circle all of the skills it took for me to achieve what I did. I might circle bridge building, delegation, emotional intelligence, and evaluation among other skills.

WIN 3 Skills	**WIN** 2 Skills	**WIN** 1 Skills
Adaptability	Adaptability	Adaptability
Analysis	Analysis	Analysis

WIN 3 Skills	WIN 2 Skills	WIN 1 Skills
Bridge building, connecting	Bridge building, connecting	Bridge building, connecting
Budgeting	Budgeting	Budgeting
Classification	Classification	Classification
Coaching	Coaching	Coaching
Competitiveness	Competitiveness	Competitiveness
Conceptualization	Conceptualization	Conceptualization
Creativity	Creativity	Creativity
Customer care	Customer care	Customer care
Decision making	Decision making	Decision making
Delegation	Delegation	Delegation
Design	Design	Design
Drive	Drive	Drive
Editing or proofreading	Editing or proofreading	Editing or proofreading
Emotional intelligence / diplomacy	Emotional intelligence / diplomacy	Emotional intelligence / diplomacy
Estimating	Estimating	Estimating
Ethics	Ethics	Ethics
Evaluation	Evaluation	Evaluation
Event planning	Event planning	Event planning
Expediting	Expediting	Expediting
Flexibility	Flexibility	Flexibility
Forward-looking orientation	Forward-looking orientation	Forward-looking orientation
Idea generation	Idea generation	Idea generation
Image creation	Image creation	Image creation
Implementation	Implementation	Implementation

WIN 3 Skills	**WIN** 2 Skills	**WIN** 1 Skills
Improvisation	Improvisation	Improvisation
Initiation	Initiation	Initiation
Initiative	Initiative	Initiative
Innovation	Innovation	Innovation
Intuition	Intuition	Intuition
Leadership	Leadership	Leadership
Listening	Listening	Listening
Mechanics	Mechanics	Mechanics
Mediation	Mediation	Mediation
Mentoring	Mentoring	Mentoring
Monitoring	Monitoring	Monitoring
Motivation	Motivation	Motivation
Multitasking	Multitasking	Multitasking
Negotiation	Negotiation	Negotiation
Observation	Observation	Observation
Optimism	Optimism	Optimism
Performance	Performance	Performance
Persistence	Persistence	Persistence
Planning and organization	Planning and organization	Planning and organization
Problem solving	Problem solving	Problem solving
Questioning	Questioning	Questioning
Record keeping	Record keeping	Record keeping
Research	Research	Research
Reading	Reading	Reading
Resilience	Resilience	Resilience
Risk tolerance	Risk tolerance	Risk tolerance
Self-Reliance	Self-Reliance	Self-Reliance

WIN 3 Skills	**WIN** 2 Skills	**WIN** 1 Skills
Sales	Sales	Sales
Speaking	Speaking	Speaking
Strategy	Strategy	Strategy
Supervision	Supervision	Supervision
Synthesis	Synthesis	Synthesis
Teaching and training	Teaching and training	Teaching and training
Team building	Team building	Team building
Teamwork	Teamwork	Teamwork
Technology	Technology	Technology
Testing	Testing	Testing
Time management	Time management	Time management
Vision	Vision	Vision
Visualization	Visualization	Visualization
Willingness to learn	Willingness to learn	Willingness to learn
Willingness to take control	Willingness to take control	Willingness to take control
Working with numbers	Working with numbers	Working with numbers
Writing	Writing	Writing

Step 4: Now go back through your answers and for each skill you circled, ask yourself if this is something you enjoy doing. For each yes answer, circle it again but this time with your red pen.

Step 5: Notice the skills you circled more than one time. If any of these are circled with a red pen, they're skills that you not only posess right now but also like using.

Step 6: Write down ten skills you both have and like in the blanks below.

1. _____

2. _____

3. _____

4. _____

5. _____

6. _____

7. _____

8. _____

9. _____

10. _____

Step 7: Put a star with your red pen next to the five skills that you think would be most satisfying for you to do on a regular basis. These five skills are going to help you build your dream.

Putting It All Together

You've done good work. You've remembered a lot about yourself and are starting to piece together how you can use what you have to advance your business in the real world. Now take the time to fill out the following at-a-glance worksheet with the answers you came up with in the previous sections so you have it all in one place to refer to when you start to wonder if you're on the right path. It is my hope that these exercises will make you surer than ever that being an entrepreneur is what you're meant to be.

PUTTING IT ALL TOGETHER

PASSIONS

LIST YOUR TOP FIVE PASSIONS, STARTING WITH THE MOST SATISFYING:

1. _____
2. _____
3. _____
4. _____
5. _____

SKILLS

LIST YOUR TOP TEN SKILLS, STARTING WITH THE MOST SATISFYING:

1. _____
2. _____
3. _____
4. _____
5. _____
6. _____
7. _____
8. _____
9. _____
10. _____

For me, when I see my passions and skills and what makes me uniquely qualified all laid out, I can't walk away from it. There has to be a reason why all these things are coming together right here. There has to be a purpose for me. All I have to do is take the leap.

I believe that for you too. It's all here. You're gifted with skills and talents and thoughts and abilities that only you have. It's time you use them. That little idea that lives in you is trying to break out. Take some time to figure out how your passions and skills might work into your business idea. I never thought my photography and writing skills would have much to do with my sales business, but they turned out to be huge assets as I created marketing strategies and connected with my audience online. How might the same be true for your individual passions and skills?

The next chapters will explore the ten success philosophies that will get you started down the path to entrepreneurship—the principles that will help you boss up in the way that's right for you and your unique situation.

You ready? Let's go.

SUCCESS PHILOSOPHY #1:
THINK LONG-TERM

The first success philosophy is to think long-term about your business right from the beginning. Failing to do this is a crucial mistake I see a lot of budding entrepreneurs* make. They jump right into the business, thinking only about what they want in the present or the near future and fail to even think about what needs to happen further down the road. But you can put yourself onto the path to disaster if you don't have a clue where you want to go over the long haul with all of your work. And even if everything turns out okay, you can waste a lot of time and money in the process.

You need to start at the beginning, get a firm grasp, and set up a foundation for your business based on your ultimate goals for yourself and your business. In other words, you have to "begin with the end in mind," as Stephen R. Covey puts it.[1] Thinking long-term now will help you be smart about every change and decision you make about your business along the way.

How you employ this strategy, however, may differ according to your personality type. If you're anything like me, you'll probably be tempted to rush through some of these first steps to get to the fun stuff—the stuff

....

* Or, as I like to call them, "wantrepreneurs."

that feels more important and official. I would really caution you against skipping ahead if you haven't taken the time to go through each of the exercises in this chapter. They are really critical to the success of your product or service.

If, however, you're *not* like me and you tend to take a lot of time making decisions, I want you to fight the instinct to overthink this. Don't sit for hours and hours thinking about the same thing over and over. Write down your thoughts and, if you need to, walk away and come back to them later. Analysis paralysis is real, and it won't help you create your best work. Set a deadline. Set a timer. Just don't sit and stare at a blank piece of paper—that's a good way to quit before you even get started.

Plan to Stand Out

Okay, so you have this idea for a product or service.

Let's imagine your idea as a car. After you assemble all the parts and put that car together, you're going to put that sucker on the road. This road is your path to success. Looking ahead, it should lead to your product or service being the best in its industry. I'm not talking about sixth place. I'm not talking about 184th place. Best means number one.

Let me be clear though. I'm not talking about you going into business as a photographer and being the most booked photographer in the world in thirteen business days. What I'm saying is look around you, consider where you want to go, and think about what will get you there. Who is your competition? What are the competing photographers doing right now? How can you spin what's standard in the industry so you get noticed? How can you make what you offer different enough so people will want to do business with you and, at some point, you become the person others look to compete with?

In other words, don't go into business without a plan to stand out and eventually be best at whatever you do.

When your business is in its infancy, thinking about being the best in an industry can feel really scary. Trust me, I would literally shake when I thought about the kind of money my business brings in now when I was just starting. I remember thinking to myself, *There's no way*. But, as things usually do, one thing leads to another, and before you know it, you're ready to hire your first employee.

I caution you against the "why even try" negative outlook that comes so easy when we're just starting out. What I want you to get out of this lesson is to think about your product and your competition. I want you to have the best chance at success, and that means taking a real hard look at the industry you're about to enter.

Perhaps you're just looking for that extra $500 like we talked about earlier. That's fine, but I find most entrepreneurs get to that first benchmark and start dreaming of what could be if it turned into $1,000. In fact, if you ask most people how much money they'd need to live their version of the good life, they will tell you they'd need to double their income. The thing is, that doesn't stop once you get to that goal; we are constantly upping our game and changing our minds about how we want to live. There's nothing wrong with that; it's what keeps me moving toward a new goal. Just because the goal is small at the beginning doesn't mean you shouldn't work to set yourself apart from the competition and come to the table with a unique vision for your product or service to be the best in the industry.

The way I did this when my product was the same as the competition was by changing the way I serviced my clients. I told them up front what they could expect from me, and I promised never to put my own needs in front of theirs. And I didn't just promise; I delivered. I treated my customers and the people who were working with me differently, and that made our team stand out. I connected with my people through what they wanted in their lives, not just what they wanted from my product.

This strategy made us more desirable. It made us trendy. And before I knew what end was up, our competition was falling all over themselves trying to beat us.

It's worth it to go into the market with a product or service that is different enough to be the best in the long term. Here's the thing: if you get your product to the number-ten spot in your market (either a specific geographical location or your online competition), that's going to be great, and you'll be happy to have that income. But you'll also constantly be chasing your competitors who do more business. A few simple changes to set you apart could create a situation where your top competitor is forced to start chasing your success by innovating.

If you look at your product or service and then look at all of the competing products out there, do you honestly believe what you want to offer can be number one in its industry? If so, you're good to move forward. But if not—and it could be for any number of reasons (not different enough, a saturated market, iffy location, pricing out of the market, or whatever), you probably need to go back to the drawing board.

You don't have to scrap the idea entirely and never chase that dream. You just have to come up with a new iteration of that original idea, one that really has the potential to get your product to number one in its market. Until you can do that, you can't say yes to your idea. There has to be a uniqueness that sets you apart from your competition.

Let me give you some examples I've seen just scrolling casually through my social media feeds.

When I last checked, there were 184,000 posts on Instagram about wooden signs. A quick Etsy search returned 165,000 results. Wooden signs are everywhere. So if you've got this great idea to make wooden signs, you're going to have to think long and hard about what is going to set your wooden signs apart from the hundreds of thousands of competitors. How can you disrupt the wooden sign industry so that you can get your product to number one in its market long-term? You want to be the best-known wooden sign company, the first Google search result. You don't want to get lost in the sea of sign makers who haven't examined their product ideas enough before jumping into the market.*

"Start small, build big" should be your focus from the very beginning if you want to be a momtrepreneur. Eventually you can hire a team to help

....

* I went to speak at an event recently, and five of the fifty entrepreneurs in attendance were wooden-sign makers. Not one of them could tell me what differentiated their product outside of font and wood type because none had thought long-term about what it would take to be number one.

you keep your product or service on the cutting edge of the market. But when you are just starting, it's up to you to set the precedent of what you ultimately want from your business.

If your goals are more modest—just making some extra money over the course of a few years, maybe to put away money for your kids' college—that's okay too. You can choose to be a freelancer instead of an entrepreneur. (I'll talk more about the distinction later in this chapter.) But this kind of thinking about what you really want out of your business is exactly what you should be doing up front, before you ever get started.

No matter what size you want to grow your business, one of your goals should be profit related. If there's no profit (after a certain point, which you get to determine*), there's no business. Give yourself enough time to actually make your business work. But if year after year you aren't able to turn a profit, something has to change. It's either going to be you shaking up how you do what you do, learning new skills to make your business better, or setting your sights on something different where you can make more of an impact on the market.

Let's look at social media apps. The number one social media app in the United States is Facebook, with 168 million users in 2018. The number ten most popular? Google Hangouts, with 15 million users. That's quite a difference. So unless I could find a way to disrupt the social media industry, I wouldn't invest my time, money, and energy developing an app to try to take down Facebook (my biggest competition). A copy of Facebook won't beat them at their game, I'd have to come up with a superior product first.

Likewise, if I want to own a retail shop geared toward mothers, I'm not going to set out to take down Target right now. Target is not in my market, Target is a huge corporation. Other boutique shops that carry a similar product line? Maybe.

Same thing with Amazon. If I own an online shop, my goal isn't to

....

* But determine wisely because you need to give yourself enough time to actually succeed. (I'm talking three to five years.) And don't you dare let me catch you giving up prematurely if this is what makes you happy.

put Amazon out of business in the next decade. Amazon didn't become what it is overnight. They got there by evolving, changing, and innovating day after day, week after week for years. It took Jeff Bezos years before he turned a profit. Maybe someday you and I can compete with Target or Facebook, but right now let's be honest about what we have the power to do as small-business owners.

I don't want to be negative here. I just don't want you to waste your time and money and energy on a product that doesn't have the potential to knock your customers' socks off and help you survive the difficult road to success. Don't put out a product that is inferior or one that's more or less the same as what's already out there. Your competition has gotten to the market first. You have to think hard about how you're going to compete successfully *before* you move in.

Turn your idea around in your head. How can you improve it? How can you give your customers something unexpected? How can you add a new feature that hasn't been seen before? Perhaps you can diversify your product offering so that you can make something new with the idea you have. Or perhaps you can change the way you deliver the product to increase customer satisfaction. Keep turning your idea around until you come up with a variation that will be the envy of your market. Then go through the same process again and again over time as you improve upon your original idea.

Try it here by answering some questions about a business you would like to start:

What is your unique vision for a product or service?

_____

How is your product different from your competition?

_____

Who is currently number one in your industry?

_____

What are some ways you could tweak or adapt your idea to make it stand out more?

PRO TIP

Do you have one creative friend who, when you give her an initial idea, cranks out new spinoff ideas right away? If you have a friend like that, let her help you talk through your idea to come up with something original.

Find Your Target

Before you go making any decisions about what to call your product (if you have decided to create your own), or how you're going to build your sphere of influence (if you have decided to sell a service or become an influencer), and then how to market your product or service, it's important that you know who you're targeting. This is the first step behind figuring out whether you can actually meet enough customers' needs to be successful. Determining your target market will set the tone for everything you do and every decision you make.

And how do you determine your target market? Think: *Who is it that I want to reach with my product or service?*

Most people assume the correct answer to this question is "everyone!" *I want everyone to buy what I have to sell.* If you think that, you're not alone. But the truth is that when you market to everyone, you market to no one. But when you narrow your focus to a more specific target, you get much better results.

Business owners who target too broad an audience—for instance, try to sell necklaces to both empty nesters and millennials—tend to lose the trust of those they reach. Their messaging isn't consistent and might not even be appropriate. The way you talk to a millennial is not likely the way you'd talk to someone who is close to retirement. So build trust with your potential customers by focusing consistently on a more specific target and marketing consistently with them in mind.

Remember that marketing to a specific type of person doesn't mean you won't get outliers—people outside the target group who still have interest in what a business is offering. There are plenty of people reading this book right now, for instance, who don't have kids yet or don't plan to have kids.* But these people will find you even when you're specific about who you're trying to reach.

When you're done with this section, I want you to have a very clear, drilled-down picture of who will buy your product and what needs you can meet by offering it. I strongly believe that the number one reason start-ups fail is a lack of market need for the product they offer. You can't make money if nobody wants to buy your product. So let's make sure that's not going to happen to your business by finding a specific target demographic that needs the product or service you want to bring to market.

The following questions about your target demographic can help you get a better sense of who she (or he) is. Try to be as specific as possible in answering them.

How old are the people you want to reach?

_____

What is their gender?

_____

List three things that interest them.

_____

....

* Hey, guys, thanks for reading this book even though you don't have little kids destroying your house right now. Well played—and if I'm honest, I'm a little bit jealous of your life right now. Cheers!

What three things do they value most?

_____

Where do they live?

_____

What is their income level?

_____

Are they married?

_____

What do they do for a living?

_____

How many hours of free time do they have in a day?

_____

What is their religious affiliation?

_____

What is their racial/ethnic identity?

_____

Do they have kids? How many?

_____

What are their hobbies?

_____

What kind of car do they drive?

_____

What is their education level?

What kind of books do they read?

Do you have a very clear picture of that one person now? Does it feel oddly specific? If so, you're on the right track. It's important to be detailed about this because all these factors will impact your target customers' purchasing decisions.

Now, take it a step further and ask yourself if the person you just identified will benefit and find value from the product or service you're thinking about creating:

- Will your product or service meet a need for them?
- Will it make their life easier?
- Will they be willing to part with some of their discretionary income in order to have it?

If you're not sure whether the answer to these questions is yes, then it's not a terrible idea to talk to some people you know who fall within your target demographic and are willing to tell you the truth. This is especially important if you are not in your target demographic. Don't just assume that people will want your product or service. Ask people who aren't emotionally attached to you if they'd purchase what you're selling.

I once walked into the offices of a fairly large company and found a cutout of my face pinned to the walls of 80 percent of the cubicles. I was a little freaked out at first until I was told that the cutouts had been given to the employees in every customer-facing role to help them put a face to the person they were interacting with. I represented the target market this company was trying to connect to. Rather than spouting off facts about the kind of person they wanted to reach, they simply handed out my picture—a physical representation of the target.

I thought it was pretty brilliant—so brilliant, in fact, that I want you to try it. Find a picture of a person who represents your target market. For extra credit, make a copy and hang it up next to your computer or wherever you work so you've always got a reminder of the person you should be talking to, the person whose needs you're trying to meet with your product or service.

Name Your Brand

The next thing you need to decide is what to call your business. It's time to give your company a name.

You've really only got two choices when it comes to brand names. You can name your company, or you can give the company your name. Will your company be called the Widget Company or Widgets by Jen? Will the name you choose be good enough to stand the test of time and keep people coming back? Here are some things to consider when creating your brand's name:

1. **Keep it simple.** How does the name sound when your customer says it out loud? Is it too hard to spell or understand? Figuring out your business name like a vanity license plate on the road is not a fun game. If people have to spend too much time trying to remember how to spell or say your company name, they're moving on to your competitor.*

2. **Make it clear.** I was given two pieces of advice early in my writing career that changed the way I look at both book titles and product names. The first piece of advice is: "Make sure the title tells the reader what your book is about in as few words as possible." The second is: "Don't expect the subtitle (or ad copy) to make up for a terrible title." The name of your product should communicate succinctly what it is and why it would benefit us as consumers. It should tell us enough that we know we're interested without

....

* Sorry, not sorry, Motorola Razr and Oscillococcinum.

reading every detail. Simple and straightforward doesn't have to mean bland and boring though. Take three minutes to browse through the names of podcasts, and you'll see what I mean. The goal is to be both clear and interesting.

3. **Pick a name that passes the "grunt test"**—author Donald Miller's name for something so simple a caveman could understand it.[2] That's what we're going for when it comes to business and product names. Ideally your brand name will mean something. That way it will be easier to understand and remember. If it is made up of initials, jargon, inside information, or words you concocted out of thin air, it's not your best idea. And that's okay; we only get to the good ideas through the bad ones. Just don't stop at the bad ideas.

4. **Make sure the name is available for you to use.** Trust me, you don't want to build a brand on a name that you can't legally use and then get a cease and desist letter demanding you change everything. You can easily search the US Patent and Trademark Office online to see whether the name you want is available.[3] Be sure to look for different versions of the name you want to use. Even if a name is legal, you don't want it to be almost the same as that of another business.

5. **Check for availability of a web address (or addresses) to go along with your new business name.** Keep in mind that the address needs to be easy enough for people to remember and enter into their browser. Since web addresses aren't terribly expensive, consider buying more than one. I recently changed my web address from lindsayteaguemoreno.com to lindsaytm.com just because it was easier for people to get right. I also bought LindseyTM.com in case people are inclined (and they are always inclined—thanks, Mom) to spell my name with an *e*. I often lie awake at night thinking of new business ideas, and when one occurs, I immediately buy the domain name to go along with it—just in case. My collection of domain names borders on crazy.*

....

* What's my worst two-in-the-morning domain decision, you ask? Possibly RichandFabulous.net. I'm ashamed on so many levels.

6. **Google your name and business concept and Google them hard.** Search all the pages that come up with your keyword in quotes. Who else is using your concept? How are people talking about what you're about to name your company? Does it make sense? What other business owners have been on the same track? Have you checked the Urban Dictionary yet? Do it because you do not want to give your business a name that may have a meaning that's better left in the Cards Against Humanity box.

7. **Test it out with people who will tell you the truth.** After you've done your research online and through other resources, test it out on people who will give you honest answers. We all have yes people in our lives who will tell us what we want to hear. Those people make us feel good temporarily but lead us astray in the long run.

8. **Pick a name that will communicate with your target market.** Don't choose one that will speak to a seventy-year-old man if your target market is a millennial of the female variety. Knowing what your target market is into and the language they speak with each other is important when naming a product. This is especially important when it comes to the play on words. Is your empty-nester target market going to connect to the word *slay* or *bae** like a twenty-three-year-old would? Probably not.

Are you getting the idea? Better yet, are some ideas coming to you? Take some time to brainstorm name ideas in the space below:

Next, write down your final pick and make sure it meets the eight considerations we looked at above.

_____

....

* Or whatever words are current by the time this book comes out!

Consider Putting Your Face to the Name

One thing you might not have considered is who will be the face of your brand. That's something else you're wise to consider when you're just starting out. The easiest and most obvious answer is you, of course. After all, it is your company.

That doesn't mean your widget company needs to put out widgets called Karen Smith with your face all over the packaging. You can still name your widgets whatever you want and package them in whatever way seems best to you.* But think about whether your ultimate goal is to be the face of the brand, if you want your face and persona to be the one people associate with your product. Your widgets might ultimately give you the platform to become an influencer, a podcaster, a speaker, or an authority figure. Your small business might pave the way for you to do so much more for the people you serve than simply provide a product. If you have the slightest desire for that—or think you might desire it in the future—your name and image should be part of your packaging and advertising from the beginning.

One of the mistakes I made when I built my sales business was creating a brand that took off without my name attached. I created the brand. I developed it. I thought through the entire process of what that brand would represent. I was the voice of that brand. And yet I didn't think enough of myself as the owner to attach my name to it.

I thought I was being humble—that putting my name on my brand sounded self-serving. Maybe I was a little afraid to put myself out there. At any rate, I didn't. So it was 100 percent my fault that people were confused when they learned I was the owner of that brand. It was my fault when people knew my brand name but had never heard of me. It is my fault still that although I'm a multimillion-dollar-producing business owner, speaker, podcaster, and educator, lots of people still don't know who I am and why they should take advice from me. I had someone in

....

* As long as the word *moist* isn't part of it, thankyouverymuch.

an interview this week tell me how hard it was to find information on me on the Internet—and that's my own fault too. I did that to myself by not thinking long-term about my naming decisions and where I was going.

The truth is, putting a face and name to a product is one of the smartest things you can do for your business. People tend to trust a person more than they do a brand name. Think about it. Why do companies often hire celebrities to hawk their products instead of unknown actors or product advocates? Because it's human nature to trust people we "know" more than we do strangers. We feel like we know Oprah, so we buy her favorite things because we believe what she tells us to do is going to be good for us. It's the reason we buy makeup from Ellen DeGeneres and watches from professional athletes. Recognizable faces and names sell stuff.

Even when a company doesn't purposely lead with a person, as consumers we naturally seek out someone we can associate with the brand. We tend to purchase from people rather than companies, and this seems especially true of online sales.

Take Apple computers for example. There's a reason people became obsessed with Steve Jobs as the company figurehead. Connecting the excellent product to a person and not an organization made us feel more connected to what was being sold. Apple didn't fully understand that when they were growing; at one point they even fired Jobs from his position at Apple . . . then gave in and hired him back. Jobs wasn't even known to be a kind, warm, or nice person, and yet people seemed to crave more exposure to him. Have you thought about why? It's because Steve Jobs is an integral part of Apple's story, and we are hardwired to want more stories in our lives. (We're going to talk about this in depth in another chapter.)

Even if you give your company a strong name, in other words, I want you to give serious thought to making your personal identity part of your brand. Don't make the mistake I did and realize too late that you are the best thing for your business when it comes to sales. Your face, your name, your personality, your voice, and your story can do a lot to convert your efforts into sales if you're willing to be brave and put yourself out there.

Define the Brand of You

There is a difference between your brand identity and your actual brand. When I talk about brand, I find that people often think of a logo, colors, and fonts. But that's brand identity, not the brand itself.

Simply put, your brand is not your logo. Your brand is what people say about your business (and you) when you're not around. It's what people feel when they interact with your website or social media accounts. One of the most important parts of getting a successful business off the ground is fully understanding every part of it. And when I say *it*, I mean *you*.

Okay, I can almost feel you cringing as you read that. I know every one of the excuses ticking through your brain right now because I've been in your shoes. Assigning characteristics, colors, and feelings to a brand you create is totally different than assigning them to yourself. Spending time and resources to highlight yourself feels really self-centered and vulnerable at the same time.[*]

As if that wasn't enough, we've been told that amazing businesses develop on their own, as if from magic, and that the best business owners don't have to promote themselves. Wrong. I call BS. That's some jacked-up narrative we've chosen to believe. If you know a company name or the business owner's name, that's almost always because the owner made that happen on purpose. There are very few exceptions to that rule.

Brands are created on purpose. And smart businesspeople create a name for themselves on purpose. They do it by serving their brand—and themselves—up to their target market over and over and over and over. It takes letting go of the idea that your brand is just going to create itself, or that the process will be easy as pie if it's right. It's going to be *easier* if it's right, but that does not mean it's easy.[**]

You have to be prepared to define yourself and make that part of your company's brand. We're talking small business here—grassroots. Your

....

[*] As moms, we're not supposed to do that, right? We're supposed to be thinking of others. All the eye-rolls, friends. All. The. Eye-rolls.
[**] What's the extreme opposite of easy? It's going to be that.

best bet for success is to get to know your customers and, more important, let them get to know you. You are the secret sauce. It's fine for large companies that are already established to put the brand before the people, but in today's social-media-driven world, you're going to have to put yourself into your brand and let people choose if they like it or not. Your brand needs personality, even if you are uncomfortable showcasing yours to build your business.

Right now, actually, we're seeing large companies move more toward the personal too. They're changing the way they interact with people because consumers are changing the way they are influenced and how they communicate. That's why we see billion-dollar companies tweeting with single customers, creating a persona on social media for their organization, and often going so far as to try to entertain us to win our loyalty. If you don't believe me, spend three minutes checking out airline and fast-food Twitter battles. Savage. And if you really want to laugh, peep the hilarious feeds of Old Spice, Taco Bell, Honda, Wendy's, Southwest Airlines, Gordon Ramsay, Pepto Bismol, and Miller Lite. Brilliant.

These days you really have no choice. You have to put yourself—the real you—in front of your audience if you want to differentiate yourself from your competition. Your customer is really buying *you* when they choose to buy a product from your small business—and, guys, the competition is fierce. There's always someone somewhere who is willing to undercut your price. So it's up to you to *be* the brand the market trusts over that bargain brand.

So how do you define your personal brand in order to fast track the trust you want the customer to give you? In the next few pages we'll outline some helpful strategies.

Brand Strategy #1: Compile a List of Brand Words

Your brand words are the ten words that best describe the tone and culture of your entire brand. Ideally they will be the aspects of yourself you choose to present to the world when you do business. Once you figure them out, they can help you keep your marketing focused, consistent, and honest.

I determined my own brand words about a year into my business, and this list has served me well. Here's a peek at how I want my brand to be known:

creative	*unique*
hilarious	*strong*
bright	*relevant*
authentic	*relentless*
innovative	*smart*

I recently surveyed my social media followers to find out what they thought about my brand. I asked them what words came to mind when they interacted with me online. What I was really after was finding out if my brand was perceived the way I wanted. What were other people *saying* about me and my product when I wasn't around?

Here were the top ten words my followers used to describe the LTM (Lindsay Teague Moreno) brand:

inspiring	*fun*
honest	*colorful*
fresh	*bright*
authentic	*boss*
powerful	*funny*

Note how similar the two lists are. To me this similarity is validation that I'm being brand consistent in my interactions with my customers.

I want this for you as well—the kind of brand consistency that says over and over, "I'm always going to be here. This is what I love. This is what I do. This is who I am. You can trust me." That trust will sell your product. And developing your own list of brand words is invaluable in helping you develop that consistency.

This exercise is really important because it sets the tone for your brand. Whether you like it or not, your audience will start to create their own lists about you and your brand unless you do it first. *You* get the chance to define what you want people to say about you and your company if you take the time to write out the words.

Here's the catch though. You have to be willing to live out these words long-term, which means they should be consistent with who you actually are on your best days. They won't necessarily define *all* of who you are, of course—no human being can be completely summed up in a short list of words. But they should still represent you. Don't choose words that you can't consistently deliver.

For instance, you may want your brand to be really funny for your customers. But if you're not the funny chick at parties, the one people laugh with (or at), that might be a little difficult to deliver on consistently. So focus instead on words that do represent you—and resist the temptation to value words that don't describe your brand (like *funny* in the example above) more than the words that actually *do* describe you (maybe *dependable* or *creative*). Focus less on what you don't offer and more on what you can deliver beautifully and consistently.

To develop your list of brand words, begin by brainstorming twenty words that describe you on your best day and that you would like to describe your business as well. I often say that my brand words are the compliments I've received throughout my life that stuck with me and made me feel the best. Those are the ways I want people to describe my brand.

_____   _____

_____   _____

_____   _____

_____   _____

_____   _____

_____   _____

_____   _____

_____   _____

Now I want you to narrow down those twenty words to ten and spruce them up a bit. Give those words some magic. Don't say *funny;* say *hilarious.* Use the word *sophisticated* instead of *fancy.* Try *rebel* instead of *different.*

These ten brand words should make your business come to life. They will help you remain consistent each time you work.

I want you to make sure you exhibit one of your brand words in each interaction you have with a customer. Make sure people can *feel* these words as they read your social media or blog posts. And post your list of words next to your workspace so you don't have to wonder if what you're about to do is brand consistent.

Write your final ten brand words below. Or, better yet, set them up in an eye-catching font, print them out, and post them where you can see them every day. They will help you keep your brand personal, authentic, and consistent.

_____   _____

_____   _____

_____   _____

_____   _____

_____   _____

Brand Strategy #2: Establish Your Core Values and Brand Principles

Core values are the fundamental beliefs of a person or a company. All decisions about and for your business should be based on what you believe to be good, true, right, and best. Your core values should infuse every fiber of your organization, products, services, and company culture from the very beginning and for years to come. When (or if) you later scale your small business and hire employees, sharing these core values will help these employees gain a strong sense of how you work and what you believe.

In 2009, Apple revealed that one of their core brand principles was to deliver an innovative product that really makes a contribution. If they're thinking about expanding a product line or developing a new product, they'll only do it if they can deliver innovation that contributes to that market. They won't expand because they want to slap the Apple logo onto something that's just a regurgitation of an existing product. Anything new has to show real innovation, and it has to contribute.[4] That's a great brand principle for the company to use as a lens for their business decisions.

Each company will have a different list of core values that sets them apart from their competition. We can all agree on a lot of things that are true and good, but they won't be in the same order of importance for each business. What I want for you to do in this section is develop a list of the core values you value most for your business. Such a list can really help when you're faced with tough questions. Applying your values list to those questions will help you know which decisions are right or wrong for your business. Your values will determine your actions.

One of my core values is to always choose authenticity above opportunity. I refuse to sell something I don't believe in, promote something I wouldn't use myself, or represent myself falsely to a customer, even if it means I don't get the same opportunities that other entrepreneurs will. Because I'm so clear about my desire for authenticity, it's easy for me to know which opportunities to pursue and which doors are just not good for me to walk through.

Let me give you an example. This week alone I got an offer to use my platform to influence my followers into buying the following products:

beef jerky

a nonprofit selling greeting cards

a social media app

an online business course

tea

custom jewelry

rental vacation properties

beef snacks (not to be confused with jerky, folks)

earrings

teeth whitening

a fashion app

gum

baby photo-booth products*

....

* Notice I'm missing the California wineries knocking down my door to send me cases of their product. (I'm looking at you, Opus One.) Must revise my strategy on this.

As I consider this list, I know right away that I'll likely never use or love some of these products (especially the beef snacks and the baby photo-booth stuff) because I'm not their target market. It doesn't matter how much I'm paid for my endorsement. I simply can't put something in front of my audience that I don't actually use and like because doing so would go against my core value of authenticity. I've never done that before, and I won't betray the trust my followers place in my recommendations by doing it now. Someone else out there will get the opportunity to do it, and I'm perfectly okay with that.

That said, some of the other items in the list could work for me, so I could try a few of these products and see if I like them. If I do, then I would consider recommending them to my audience, but I won't promise a post on any product without trying it and knowing it's for me.

Listing your own core values might take a little time and thought, but it's really worth attempting. Do a little brainstorming (and soul searching) and try to come up with a list of ten core values for your business. They should of course reflect your own personal values as well. Once you have these written down, it becomes so much easier to communicate the culture of your business to your customers and to your future employees. If you get stuck, start by picking a few value words and build the value statement around it.

To get you started, here are a few of my business values:

1. We believe in authenticity above opportunity.
2. We put a unique twist on every LTM product we produce.
3. We are relentless in the search for needs we can meet.
4. We know that trust is the foundation of our success, and we will strive to be a brand our customers can put their trust in.
5. We believe that a positive environment provides the best opportunity to learn and grow.
6. We believe that autonomy produces the best work.
7. We work in a way that promotes curiosity and more questions.
8. We prioritize fun in and out of the office.
9. We believe in the power of bright colors and quirky one-liners.

Write your own list below:

———————————————————————

———————————————————————

———————————————————————

———————————————————————

———————————————————————

———————————————————————

———————————————————————

———————————————————————

———————————————————————

Brand Strategy #3: Determine Your Brand Promise

A brand promise is a statement that tells your customers what they can expect if they choose your product over that of the competition—and trust me, there's always another way your customers could be spending their money. This promise will tell them the kind of principles your company is founded on and show why your product is the safest choice for their money.

Here's an example of a brand promise we've probably all heard. "Fifteen minutes or less could save you 15 percent or more on car insurance." Geico gets right to promising you what you should expect if you decide to check out their product. They're promising to save you money in less time than it would take to get a coffee.

To determine your brand promise, you need to tap into the core values you listed in the previous exercise. Now is your chance to think through how you're going to put these values into action, giving your customers a product or service to really believe in. Some questions you might ask yourself include:

- Will you pride yourself on giving the best customer service to your customer?
- Will you have a guarantee on your product that promises it will work for a certain amount of time or the customer's money will be refunded?
- Will you promise to beat your competition's price?
- Will you make sure customers will get what they paid for within a certain number of business days?
- Will you be the company that always thinks ahead and innovates?
- Will you think about the environment when it comes to packing and shipping?

Try to be creative in thinking about the things you can promise your future customer so they feel all warm and fuzzy about what they're spending their money on. That's how I feel when I spend my money at my favorite coffee joint, Dutch Bros. Coffee. When I leave there, I am actually glad to part with my money and happy to have the product (and great service) they provide. Dutch Bros. has three brand promises that they consistently deliver. Go buy one, and you'll be as convinced as I am. Their brand promises are:

1. One cannot be sacrificed for another.
2. All must work together to provide the best experience possible.
3. We may be a coffee company, but we are in the relationship business.

A brand promise is something you consistently deliver to the customer so they know they can trust you with their hard-earned time and resources. Once your business starts rocking and rolling, you can come back to this list to make sure they're promises you can actually provide your customer and follow through with.

Write your possible brand promise below:

_____

_____

_____

_____

_____

Brand Strategy #4: Articulate Your Unique Selling Proposition

The last step in defining your brand is to write a statement that sums up for your customers who you are and why you're different. This is called a unique selling proposition (USP). Your USP represents the special thing you can offer that your competitors can't. It's your competitive edge. It's the reason customers buy from you and you alone.

Let me give you some examples of great USPs by successful brands:

- Toms Shoes: "Toms shoes are quirky, comfy, light, and inexpensive."
- FedEx: "When it absolutely, positively has to be there overnight."
- Target: "Expect more. Pay less."
- BMW: "The ultimate driving machine."
- M&Ms: "The milk chocolate melts in your mouth, not in your hand."
- DeBeers: "A diamond is forever."

You'll notice that most of these USPs are also used as brand slogans. That's okay. Just be careful to not let your USP become something you throw out just because it's catchy. Instead, use it as your rock to stand on.

When I was working to create my USP, I spent hours thinking through what was really important to me. I kept asking myself, _What is one thing I consistently deliver that other people in the female entrepreneurship space are missing?_ As I thought about this, I decided that it's my desire to deliver hard truths with love and humor so future female entrepreneurs are armed for the battle of growing their businesses. After all, a lot of people teach business building, but not many talk about the really messy parts of entrepreneurship or do so in a way that's entertaining. I want to be a different kind of leader in this space—one who sits in the trenches with my tribe and makes them laugh. That's what makes me unique. So here's what I came up with for my USP: *The kick in the pants you need to build the business you want.*

So consider your own future business. What will your competitive edge be? What can you offer that most people can't? It's important for you to spend quality time thinking about what's important to you and what sets you apart and then crafting your statement as succinctly and powerfully as possible.

Your USP is going to be your sales pitch. It's the thing you'll say when people ask you what your business does. If your product or service is similar to someone else's, your USP will clarify what makes your product or service stand out. And remember that you're writing this statement for your customers' benefit. It should delight your customers, rather than try to convince your skeptics.

Here are some questions to help you drill down what you need to include in your USP:

- What need do you plan to meet for your customers?
- What will make your widget different than her widget?
- What makes you most excited about selling your product or service?
- What kind of energy or culture do you want your company to have?
- What do you want to accomplish?
- What will motivate your customers to buy your product or service?
- Why will your customers need you?

Use your answers to these questions as a jumping-off point for brainstorming the things that make you and your business outstanding, then write down your USP here:

_____

_____

_____

_____

Defining Your Boundaries

Before we move into the theory and practice of meeting the needs of your target market, I want to take a minute to talk about the boundaries. Setting up clear boundaries for yourself and for your business is one of the most important ways to think long-term.

I made the mistake of not understanding this fully before making a name for myself on social media, and I paid the price. To a people pleaser (like my daughter) or to someone who cares what people they don't know think about them (like me), boundaries can feel a little cold or mean or scary. Trust me, I get it. I want people to like me and what I provide, and it bothers me when people say mean things to me online. Yes, it comes with the territory. Yes, it will happen to you at one point. Yes, it does hurt. And, no, I still haven't completely figured out how not to care what other people think about it.

However, I now understand the importance of setting really clear boundaries for you personally and for your business—knowing your priorities and what you are and are not willing to do. Ideally, that's something you should do at the very beginning.

Again, I learned this the hard way. When I first started my business, nothing was off limits. I'd find myself working all hours of the night, doing things free of charge for people just so I'd be of value to them. This was great for everyone, except me and my family. What it earned me was people who came to depend on me for free resources and for help doing their jobs. So much so that I sometimes still get e-mails from angry team members about what I'm not doing for them. I created an entitlement monster. It also earned me a strain on my relationships and a big case of burnout. So I had to set limits on what I was willing to do.

You better believe doing that brought me some real push-back. People were used to getting things from me for free at any hour of the day. They were used to saying "jump" and having me respond with "how high?" And they did not respond well when I finally said no!

Why did I agree to do those things in the first place? I honestly thought it was the right thing to do—you know, servant leadership. Also, I thought it was the only way to build a following. I didn't know that setting boundaries around my time and what I had to offer was even an option. But I know now, and I'm doing my very best to be firm about my limits.

I'm still all about servant leadership, and I'm going to talk a lot about it in this book. But now I understand that servant leadership doesn't mean you can never say no or protect yourself.

Intentional boundaries are about weighing what you can give and where you're not willing to compromise when it comes to your time, money, and energy. And I'm going to say outright that setting them is hard for me. I still struggle in this area because I discount my own health and happiness in the interest of being liked. I'm better about boundaries now than I was four years ago, but it's still a challenge for me. So I don't expect you to be really excited about the idea of saying no to people on a regular basis.

I hope you will do it anyway.

Let me also state a few facts before we get into setting boundaries:

1. Saying no is not only good for you and your business; it's a requirement.
2. Saying no frees you up to say yes to the things that are important to you.
3. Other people's opinions on what you should or should not do are likely based on what they want from you and not what is best for you.
4. You cannot please everyone, even if you do say yes to every opportunity, request, or need that comes your way.
5. Your boundaries allow you to live the life you want while building your business at the same time.

Taking these facts into consideration helped me establish the non-negotiable rules by which I now run my business:

1. I will not use my platform as a way to influence others to buy a product without having loved that product first, and I will be honest in my reviews of products I love and do not love.
2. I will not use my platform as a way to share charity needs, calls to action, or fund-raising opportunities for a person or organization I don't already support with my personal giving budget.
3. I will not reply or respond to heated religious or political conversation on social media.
4. I will not do more work than the person asking a favor of me.
5. I will not work for free, even for "exposure." My hourly rate is the same for speaking, appearance, writing, influencing, and coaching.
6. I will value the time and work of others and pay for services and products I need for my business to run.
7. I will share the imperfect version of myself online and in person.
8. I will read all comments, messages, and e-mails addressed to me, even if I must recruit help to respond to each individual message.
9. I will not work during time reserved for my family and friends—including days off and vacations.
10. I will delete (without response) comments, messages, or e-mails that are disrespectful or hurtful.

The great thing about having a list like this is that it makes my decisions for me. When someone asks me to coach them for free, my boundaries list tells me that's not something I'm willing to do. When someone asks me to share their cousin's friend's boyfriend's GoFundMe link and story, I can easily choose my answer because I don't use my platform for those kinds of sharing opportunities, even when the cause is a good one. When someone blows me up on social media because she's having a bad day and feels her opinion needs to be handled publicly, I can easily delete the post without worry—my feed, my choice, my boundary.

As you consider the five facts I listed about boundaries, take the time to consult a few key people in your life as well. Sit down with those who will be sharing time with your business as you decide the time-related boundaries. If you share money with another person in your household, set boundaries regarding money together.

Again, thinking long-term, consider: What measures will you need to take to protect yourself from burnout? What boundaries do you need to protect yourself from falling out of love with your business or product? Consider boundaries as a tool to keep you interested and engaged with your business long-term, not just when it's new and exciting.

So what do you think some of your boundaries should be—given your particular personality and circumstances? In the space below, list at least five rules you might set for yourself:

_____

_____

_____

_____

_____

_____

_____

Plan to Scale

The final thing to consider as you're planning and starting your business is a plan to scale it so you can eventually retire from it. As excited as you are to get started, let's be honest: we can't and won't work forever. Retirement can be a great thing, and it's something I personally look forward to, but I need a plan to get there. If I want to retire off of the business I'm building now, then I need a plan to keep the business running and enjoy the fruits of my labor long past the days when I'm busting my butt to get everything done. And so do you.

I often see business owners confuse the terms *entrepreneur* and *free-lancer*. There's a difference between the two, and it's an important one to understand. Entrepreneurs are business owners who have a plan to scale their business so that eventually the work won't rely on the owners. Freelancers, on the other hand, are business owners whose business depends on them to complete the work. If you are a photographer with no plan to hire, train, and mentor someone to eventually take your place as the service provider under your business name, you're a freelancer, not an entrepreneur. But if you're the owner of a boutique doughnut shop who has a plan to franchise or hire a replacement for yourself in the shop, you're an entrepreneur.

I'm super loyal when it comes to hiring services. My husband and I have used the same car service in Colorado since we moved here almost four years ago. The owner of the service, Emily, knows us by name because we've used her company every time we travel and whenever we have events to go to in our area—concerts, sports events, parties—where we might have drinks. When we first started using Emily, she did all of the driving for her business—as well as purchasing the car, setting up her website, and maintaining her schedule. At that point Emily was a freelancer. Eventually, though, Emily created a plan to scale her business. She partnered with other driving services and hired employees to do the actual driving while she handled the operations side of the car service. Emily is now an entrepreneur, and eventually, if her business continues to grow, she will be able to hire someone to take over her position as the controller so she can completely retire and live off of the continuing income from the business she built.

An ability to make money in my sleep is so important to me.

I won't take on any business that I can't eventually work myself out of—except when it comes to writing, speaking, and podcasting. Those are freelance jobs I love and will continue to do myself. But I have a plan to scale each of my other businesses until I'm no longer needed in the day-to-day schedule and will still get paid.

So that's something else to think about when you're considering the long-term implications of your business. Do you have a plan to scale it so you can eventually work yourself out of a job? Or do you love what you do so much that you always want to be part of the daily operations?

In other words, will you be an entrepreneur or a freelancer?

If you answered "entrepreneur," let's talk about what this might look like. The following questions can help:

How long do you think it will take to reach the point where you can retire from the business?

_____

How many hours do you want to work in the business in the future, and how many hours do you want to hire out?

_____

Who might you hire to take your place on the front line of your business once you retire from it? (Write down specific individuals or job descriptions or both.)

_____

What milestones in your business will let you know it's time to start thinking about phasing yourself out of the daily operations? Hint: this is likely profit related.

_____

While having a plan to phase yourself out of the operations of your business is an important part of planning your business and looking toward retirement, actually retiring from a business can prove extremely difficult to act upon when the time comes. This has certainly been the case for me. It is really hard for this control freak to trust other people with my "babies."

Building a business feels like raising a child to me: both take a lot of time, attention, blood, sweat, and tears. Both are important and become a part of me. And I have a tendency to believe that nobody will be able to care for either one the way I can. I'm not alone in that feeling, right? The thought of letting someone else make that video, plan that event, create that product, or talk to that customer is scary and a little threatening.*

The truth is, however, that there are plenty of capable and competent

....

* It's like the feeling I got when Michael and I sat down to create our will and trust. The thought of someone else taking over the parenting role for our kids is terrifying.

people out there who can do a great job for your company and even eventually replace you. It may not look exactly the same, but your baby will be safe in their hands if you do a great job creating a strong foundation and you hire the right people. And it really does help to make a plan for retirement early on, as you're building your business, so you know where you're eventually headed.

Don't Skip the Foundation

This chapter has covered a lot, and it may feel like a lot of work to figure out all these pieces and think long-term about your business before you actually start making money from it or even operating it.

And you're right. It *is* a lot of work.

It's also really important.

All of these steps together will help you create a business plan that will guide you as you make decisions. This plan is the foundation for your business, and it's important to take that foundation seriously because you can't get back the many, many hours you will put into building your business.* So let's do as much as we can to make our businesses successful from the start by following these steps and thinking long-term.

And if that wasn't enough to make you go back and go through the steps and exercises in this chapter before moving forward, then allow me to mom you right now: "If you skipped any of what you just read in this last chapter, you'd better go back and do it before moving forward. Just do it!"

....

* The money you may be able to earn back, but there's no making up for lost time.

5

SUCCESS PHILOSOPHY #2: BE UNAPOLOGETICALLY YOURSELF

My friend Anni is beautiful, fun, ambitious, extremely caring, confident, and magnetic. That comes across when you meet her in person, but it seldom comes across through her social media posts—which tend to be filled less with her big personality and more with simple facts.

Anni is a part of the generation just before mine for whom social media is just not "normal." In fact, she calls herself an "Instagrammy" because she has so many questions about how to use social media properly. She's very successful in her business, but her sales come more from pounding pavement and talking to people face-to-face. For Anni and many others like her, there's a certain fear of connecting to people through social media because it doesn't seem genuine to her. She doesn't want to expose the real her to people she isn't connecting with in person. I can understand that, given how much of social media today feels completely fake. But that fakeness we feel doesn't change unless *we* change it.

It's time for you to get comfortable sharing the real you—even on social media. This is so important that I will use an entire chapter trying to convince you of it. We're going to tackle everything from understanding your customers' emotional connection to your brand to understanding and sharing your motivation with your tribe (which is a fancy way to say followers).

Stop Apologizing

The first step to letting your freak flag fly is to stop apologizing for who you are. Stop apologizing for success. Stop apologizing for taking up time. Stop apologizing for failure. Stop apologizing for owning a space in the world.

As women, are we not in the habit of apologizing for everything? Why?

I get a lot of e-mails. I'd say 50 percent of them contain an apology of some sort for taking my time. You don't need to apologize for going after what you want.

After I do public speaking, I always hang around to look people in the eye and talk to them. I love meeting the people who are a part of my online tribe. Because God is crazy, a line usually forms so that people can take a picture or ask questions. I am both floored and humbled at times like this. I often worry that I'm wasting the time of those people who stand in line to see me because I know that the real me is really flawed and doesn't have all the answers. Then I remember that I've done everything I can to be the real me with these people online, through my books, and through my speaking—so it's the real me they want to connect with in person, too, flaws and all. It feels good to have that kind of relationship with my tribe.

That same line, however, is usually filled with women apologizing for taking up space. "Thanks for staying to talk to me. I'm sorry I'm adding to the line." They apologize for being nervous. They apologize for being excited. There's nothing we women won't apologize for. Heck, I even find myself apologizing for using an armrest on a plane—as if I don't have the same right to it as the dude sitting to my right.

The 2018 US Open tennis final featured a match between Serena Williams, a twenty-three-time Grand Slam singles title winner and one of the greatest athletes on the planet,[*] and Naomi Osaka, a twenty-year-old rising tennis star who had looked up to Serena Williams for years. A whole mess of controversy arose in that game when Williams was penalized for receiving coaching. After the match her coach admitted to the infraction. But during the match, Serena lost her ever-loving mind on the court—smashing a racket to pieces, demanding an apology from the umpire, receiving a point deduction for calling the umpire a "thief," and ultimately receiving three other violations and a $24,000 fine after having her point deducted.

Williams's behavior on the court was not that of a person who knows how to lose with grace, and it was difficult to watch. But even more painful was Naomi Osaka's reaction to winning the match. When Williams was outplayed by Osaka that day and lost fair and square—not because of deductions or penalties or anything else—the crowd took it hard and started to boo during the trophy ceremony.

Osaka took it hard as well. My insides started to twist for this young athlete standing there, about to be presented her first Grand Slam championship cup. She looked so defeated after that huge win, and when she was handed the mic, she began to cry. I thought she'd say something about how she'd dreamed of that day and how hard she'd worked for it, or perhaps she would thank her coach and family. Instead, Osaka said, "I'm sorry it had to end like this. I want to say thank you for watching the match." Then she hung her head, and the tears fell.

My mouth fell open. *Did she just apologize to the world for beating the greatest athlete on this planet? Did she actually say she was sorry for winning?*

Ladies, this has to stop.

If you've felt the need to apologize for yourself or your wins, here's your virtual hug because that ain't right.

We're done with that.

Apologies are for when we realize we've done something wrong and caused harm to another person. It's something we say to right the wrong if we can, then we work to not let history repeat itself. But Osaka did not

....

[*] In my opinion, Serena is *the* greatest athlete, followed closely by Katie Ledecky, Tom Brady, and LeBron James.

cause personal harm to anyone by beating the greatest athlete in the world. She had nothing to apologize for. And often neither do we.

Hear me, women: We should not apologize for being who we are and for being a part of this world. We shouldn't apologize for asking for what we want. We shouldn't apologize when we win or when we lose because those things don't harm other people (even if they want to feel victimized by you).

This is a self-confidence problem. We don't believe we have as much of a right to exist in the business world (or in the world in general) as other people, so we apologize for ourselves.

Self-confidence is the secret weapon to your business success. Be unapologetically who you are.

Be strong enough to like what you like.

Be confident enough to say what you mean.

Take up space.

Be too loud.

Be too much.

Be you, and don't apologize for it.

You didn't do someone wrong by being yourself. Stop believing you owe another human being an apology for existing.

Lift your head high, direct your eyes above the foreheads of everyone in the room, and exist on purpose.

When you do these things, your true self shines, and people want to be a part of that.

Does that mean that you'll be right for everyone? No, it absolutely does not. But you will resonate with a lot of people if you have the confidence to show up as you are and put the real you on the line.

Building a Genuine Connection

I want you to think about the times you've built a relationship with someone. Think back on any of those moments in that relationship where you felt a genuine connection to the other person. When I first met my husband, it took me a few dates to really feel that spark with him. We were both coming out of really long relationships and, to be honest, neither of us was very good at dating because we hadn't done much of it.

Then one day Michael took me to happy hour at an Applebee's restaurant,* where we bonded over half-price appetizers and cheap beer. More important, we met up with a friend of his, and I got to observe how he interacted with someone he knew well. Finally I was seeing the genuinely kind and laid-back person he really is, and fireworks went off inside of me. When he let himself be vulnerable enough to reveal the real him, we were able to connect.

This same idea applies to interacting with customers. People just want a glimpse of the real. They want to be able to connect to the actual person behind the brand. That's what builds trust, loyalty, and relationships with the people we work with. That's the thing that sells. It's not the flashy product, beautiful pictures, perfect lifestyle, gorgeous hair, or perfect words. Your customer wants to see the real you. They want to know they can trust you because if they can trust you, they can trust your business—and they will buy what you're selling.

Note that this works both for face-to-face customers and those on the Internet. If you're like my friend Anni, who I mentioned at the start of this chapter, the Internet can feel like a scary place. Yet the Internet is where the people are these days. Take advantage of it. Meet your customers where they are at—and for most of us, it's on social media. Be who you are and let people like that person even if you don't know them in real life. I promise that showing the real you online won't take away from the real friendships you have in your life.

Don't Build Your Brand on a Lie

To say I was invested in Lance Armstrong's phenomenal career as a cyclist would be a lie. But my husband, on the other hand, was really invested.

....

* Because where else do you take the girl you're trying out for marriage material?

Michael wore his bright yellow LIVESTRONG bracelet each day when we were dating. He read Armstrong's memoir, *It's Not about the Bike,*[1] and closely followed his career. He especially admired Armstrong for competing and winning against those disgusting blood dopers* within the sport and for staunchly defending himself when he was accused of doing the same. After all, who doesn't believe the innocence of a man who's willing to pursue legal action against his accusers? Of course he must be innocent! He survived cancer, for God's sake, and still won the Tour de France like 274 times!**

Michael, like so many others, believed in Lance Armstrong and what he stood for and felt inspired by him. That is, until the day when Armstrong got caught blood doping himself. You would have thought someone had broken up with Michael that day—he was that upset about it. He had defended his hero to me countless times during our marriage, and now he had to admit he and so many others had believed a lie.

You know who sold my husband that lie? Lance Armstrong did. Michael felt betrayed, and he wasn't the only one. To this day many people feel personally victimized by that lie. Michael read me an article about a recent trip of Armstrong's to Denver, where a whole restaurant patio full of people started yelling "eff you" at the cyclist as he was trying to catch an Uber.[2]*** And yes, it was ridiculous for grown people to yell at someone this way. But the lie Armstrong told these people had to have hurt them deeply for them to have such a strong reaction.

Now keep in mind that Lance Armstrong didn't kill other people. He's not a murderer. He's not a rapist. He didn't join ISIS. He was an athlete who replaced his old blood with fresh, new blood when he competed. But he lied about it, and that lie hurt a lot of people along the way

....

* Blood doping is injecting oxygenated blood into an athlete before a contest to improve performance. It's considered cheating in the cycling world, and it's illegal— even though every competitor does it, and I don't understand this sport, and it is stupid. Gluten-free opinions, comin' atcha.

** This may be an exaggeration on actual facts, but it was a lot of times.

*** In case you're wondering, they didn't actually say "eff you." I'm told writing the F-word is a real no-no when it comes to books. Who knew?

by ruining their reputations and careers. The lie is the thing his fans feel personally victimized by. He broke trust with his ambassadors—the people buying his stuff, contributing to his charity, and following his career.

Scott Davis, an expert in business growth, said in an article regarding Lance Armstrong, "This is one brand that is beyond repair—and I'm in the business of trying to find brand hope, often when hope is hard to find. . . . Armstrong destroyed the very values that defined him."[3] At one point during his yellow jersey days, Armstrong's brand was worth in excess of $20 million a year. Today that brand is almost worthless because the trust that supported it is gone.

This is the perfect example of how a brand is so much more than a service or a line of products. Customers will have an emotional connection to your brand, and that human connection is more than just your product or your service. There may come a time where someone will put you on a pedestal because of the brand you created, and they'll make up stories about who you are and what you're like.

That can be difficult to manage because you can only be who you are. So don't give the Internet a reason to believe you're anything other than who you are right now. Be careful to build your brand on the true you, not a lie. It's so much easier to just be who you are and let people take it or leave it. You won't be for everyone. Not everyone will like the real you. But not everyone will like the fake version of you, either.

You can build a whole business and following on a false reality. I see it every single day. You can pretend to have it all together, to look like a supermodel with a perfect life—and people will follow that. They'll even write you great comments like, "How do you do it all?" and "I wish I had your life." They'll follow you for the lifestyle they wish they had, and they'll connect to a version of you that doesn't exist.

But if you go that route, I'd suggest crossing your fingers, knocking on wood, and praying that nothing goes wrong to disrupt the version of perfect you've presented as reality—because any kind of problem you encounter will probably take down that house of cards. The Internet is fickle, and they will turn on you quickly if they've believed a lie and they know you fed it to them. In fact, many will be rooting for you to fail because they've compared themselves to your version of perfect and haven't measured up. So your failure will make them feel better about themselves, but it won't make them follow you or buy from you.

Unless you're really, really lucky or a sociopathic-caliber liar, building your business brand on lies or misrepresentation is a formula for your downfall. Besides, it isn't really necessary because—I'll say it again—you really are enough. You can build a social media following and a brand based on a genuine connection to your audience by simply being who you are and talking about the things that make up your world—including your failings, flubs, and foibles.

Leveraging Your Strengths

There are a couple of common reasons why people don't reveal their true selves to their customers in order to sell their products. One I hear all the time when I talk to female entrepreneurs is that they don't have the "right stuff" to build a winning business. They tell themselves stuff like, *If only I was better at writing, then my business would be awesome,* or *If I only knew how to do that, then I'd be successful.* The one that hits the closest to home is, *If I was thinner, people would want to follow me.*

The problem is that, as a whole, women don't sufficiently value the strengths and skills that we have. Instead, we tend to value the strengths we *don't* have. Rather than thinking of ways to use what we are good at to advance our careers, we sit around wishing we were different. We waste our time wanting to be more like someone else or something other than we are.

In chapter 4 we talked about finding the intersection of what you love (your passion) and the things you're good at (your skills, talents, and abilities). That intersection is where your strengths lie. Try revisiting those qualities here, and think especially about how you can use them right now to make your business better.

Strength	Use

Good. Now you've pinpointed five ways you can use what you have to advance your business right now. You don't need to do anything extra to use what the good Lord gave you. These are the strategies you can fall back on when you start to doubt your ability to be successful.

I'm not saying you won't have to learn new skills along the way or find people to help fill in the gaps. You will probably need to do both at some point. But the only way to know you need help or improvement is to inventory your strengths. And once you have a sense of your strengths, why not put them to work right away?

Too often I've seen business owners hold themselves back until they have everything figured out, have all their ducks in a row, and they're an expert in everything they need to run the business. Guess when that's going to happen? Exactly never. They're never going to get to that point, and they're self-sabotaging their business from the beginning by not valuing what they have right now.

Plenty of Pie

The other thing I see many entrepreneurs do that hurts their business is fall into the comparison-jealousy pit. We swallow the lie that *She's got what it takes, and I don't. My real self doesn't measure up when I compare my business to hers.*

I probably should add that I see this all the time because I find myself doing it all the time. Even with all my success and the accolades, I find myself jealous of other people's accomplishments, and that leads me to compare myself to everyone else. *What am I doing wrong?* I think. *What does she have that I don't? It's not fair; I've worked hard too.* That kind of negative self-talk and self-sabotage doesn't go away when you hit some mythical success benchmark. You won't ever be free of it unless you make a conscious and ongoing effort to be free of it.

I think we often get it into our heads that when another entrepreneur (specifically a female entrepreneur) wins or gets a taste of success, her success reflects poorly on our own success. That couldn't be further from the truth. Her success is not your failure. Her success is hers and your success is yours. Even if they don't happen on the same day.

When I start to feel like this, I make it a point to call my most grounded friend. She's not the friend who always tells me what I want to hear. She's the one who will understand how I'm feeling and then also tell me the truth. She'll always hit me with that truth bomb: "Lindsay, there's room for you here too."

Do you have a friend like that? If not, find her. If you have the guts, ask her to smack you with the truth when you need it. (But you cannot be mad when she tells you truth you don't want to hear. Remember, she's simply following your request.)

It's easy to fall into thinking of success as a pie with a limited number of pieces. So when someone gets a piece of success pie, we assume there's less to go around for the rest of us. What if we don't get any at all? We start to work from a place of desperation, thinking that success is scarce, and we panic. That's when we find ourselves getting angry at other people for having what we want so badly for our businesses. Before we know it, we're slipping into a jaded place and getting in our own way.

If success is indeed a pie, it's a huge one with unlimited pieces— enough to go around. Each of us has a slice waiting for us, and each slice tastes different based on the kind of success each of us is after. Your piece is there. It's waiting for you if you're willing to work for it. Nobody else can take it from you. You just need to stay focused on what you're doing and not what others are doing.

When you approach your business with that in mind, you can be happy for your sisters when they win. Celebrate with them. Encourage them genuinely. Think of what they must be feeling right now and remind yourself that you'll be there soon. Your colleagues and competitors have paid their own dues in their own way, and it's their turn to get some of that payoff. If you pay your dues, your time will come.

I promise you that this abundance mentality will do a whole lot more for your own happiness and success than getting caught up in scarcity thinking. Whenever you find yourself falling into jealousy and comparison, try to visualize that unlimited pie and imagine how sweet your own special slice will taste.

Get Your Head Right

Entrepreneurship is a mental game. You've got to get your head right, or you'll never be able to enjoy your work and feel accomplishment. And here's the reality you need to get into your head:

You—the real you, flaws and all—are the key to your business success. *You.*

The real you.

Not the made-up version of you that you think is worthy of success.

Not the pretend you that you've decided is cooler than the real you.

Not the you that you think you have to be so people will follow you.

Not the you that is twenty-five pounds lighter and has great skin.

Not the you who manages to do everything you need to do without breaking a sweat.

Not the version of you that makes more money.

Just *you.*

The real *you.*

The right now *you.*

It's so much easier to build your customer base and your social media following based on this real you. People will connect to that imperfect you because you're brave enough to put yourself out there. They'll follow your example, and you'll have the chance to genuinely help and change lives. They'll buy what you're selling because they know you've been honest about the hard things in your life and find it easy to believe you're honest about your product as well.

Another advantage is you won't have to worry about any surprise revelations if (or when) the truth slips out. You won't have to worry about the Internet outing your imperfections because you've already put them out there. Your failures and flaws aren't a secret shame. They're a rock for you to stand on and build something new. And that, my friends, is power.

So don't fall into the trap of starting a business based on being someone you are not and then find yourself pigeonholed into being that person each time you interact with work people in real life. It's so tempting and easy on social media. I've seen it so many times, and it breaks my heart. Just be who you are and let the people who would genuinely like you and the value you bring to them be your tribe. Don't waste your time on the people who don't. There will be both no matter what you do.

Don't build your business on a lie. Build it on you, and let your real tribe form around you. Those are the people who are going to buy from you. They're the people who are going to give you the buy-in you need to create a business that pulls in profit.

So be brave.

Speak up. Let your guard down. Unfurl that freak flag.

I promise you won't regret it.

SUCCESS PHILOSOPHY #3:
TELL STORIES AND CONNECT
THROUGH FEELING

I first met Michael Moreno at an Arizona State University football game. From that moment, it was instantly clear to me that we were opposite human beings. He was quiet, and I was, well, not quiet. He seemed to have it all together and owned his own home, while I was in a place where I lived with my mom like a boss.*

Still, he seemed nice, so I said yes when he asked me out. Soon we were dating, but I couldn't shake the feeling that something was missing. Even after that Applebee's date I described in the previous chapter, it felt like I wasn't getting the real Michael show when we were together.

Not one to keep my thoughts and desires inside when it came to my dating life, I let Michael know: "Hey, I need you to just be you and stop being so nervous around me. Can you just be the version of you that you

....

* To be fair, those were just a few character-building months for me, when I worked two jobs to save for my own place and to keep my mind off the fact that I was living back at home with Mom as a grown adult.

really are so we can see if this is actually going to work for us? Because, if not, I have to move along. You're hot, but you're too nice."

True story! I just said what I needed to say. And in a truly un-Michael move, he responded by telling me he wasn't going to let me walk away. He asked me to give him some time to open up a bit.[*]

On our next date Michael and I got into a conversation about embarrassing stories, and he told me—in detail—a story that forever changed the way I thought about him. He convinced me to go from "this probably won't work because I'm going to steamroll this poor man" to "I'm marrying this dude"[**] in just a few minutes. Allow me to share with you the story that sold me a marriage. It's the best story in this book, so buckle up.

The story goes that when Michael was around twenty years old, he went to dinner with his mom and his older sister to a Mexican restaurant near where they lived in Arizona. The thing about Mexican food in Arizona is that it's everywhere, even in strip malls. And this particular night they had decided to give this strip-mall restaurant the green light. Already, I can feel that some of you know where this may be going based on my key words, *Mexican food* and *strip mall* in the same sentence. You're right, but it's so much worse than you're thinking.

Following dinner, which I can only imagine was a real winner, Michael's mom and sister decided to hit up the Target nearby. They asked if he'd like to come in with them, and because he's a guy and doesn't understand the miracle that is Target, he opted to sit in the car and wait the seven hours it would take (he assumed) for his mom and sister to finish their shopping.[***]

Michael then proceeded to pull out his man card, set it on the dash of the car, and park in the one parking space that was zoned in a different city. Do your husbands do this? *Why?* Why are they parking five football fields away from the entrance when there's a perfectly good space within

....

[*] Ladies, you'd hang on after a line like that, right? Hot.
[**] Somebody find me a justice of the peace and a white dress because It. Is. On.
[***] I get it. I can legit spend hours in my local Target even if I already know every item that is in the store. And I do. Please don't judge me.

spitting distance of the store. I do not understand this phenomenon, but I'm told I'm not the only one.

Anyway, about three minutes after his family enters the store, Michael experienced an old familiar feeling, one we've all felt at one time or another—that sudden drop in the gut, followed by cramping that feels like the jaws of life are ripping out your insides. It's a feeling you really don't want when you're sitting in a car miles away from a bathroom.*

When the situation went from a minor issue to DEFCON 6 in three-and-a-half seconds, Michael knew he had two choices.

Choice one: He could sit in the car and let what was about to happen, happen. He could then face his mother and sister and try to explain it all on the way home, which was thirty minutes away. (Can you even imagine that car ride home?)

Choice two: he could slide out of the car and make a run for the doors of Target, where a bathroom awaited.

He picked choice number two and did the butt-clench-knees-together run toward the store. Sweat was dripping down his bright red face as he finally reached the door to the Target bathroom.

Now, I don't know about you, but when you really have to go and your brain locks in on a bathroom, things get really serious. Your body knows it's go time, and you're powerless to stop what's about to happen.

Michael was frantically undoing his belt and pants as he kicked open the stall door. He turned around without even thinking about locking the door and bent at the waist to pull down his drawers. But before he could make the transition from bending to sitting, his body pulled a move that I lovingly refer to as wall splatter.

He looked back in sheer panic and then relief as he noticed that there was a clean break and not a spot had gotten on him. At least he didn't think it had.

At this point in the story Michael was telling me, I was crying with laughter, imagining the whole thing going down. But it didn't end there. No ma'am.

....

* He did this to himself.

As Michael told it, he now realized he had another two choices.

Choice one: he could stay in the stall and attempt a cleanup.

Choice two: he could pull a switcheroo and move to the next stall to finish his business and check out the damage.

Because the prospect of choice one threatened to send him into a full-blown panic attack, he went with choice two. With his pants around his ankles, he shuffled over into the next stall. He was making sure there was no shrapnel to be found on his clothes when, at that very moment, like a gift from Jesus, the guy who *used* to clean the bathrooms at Target walked into the room.

It took three seconds for Michael's worst nightmare to become a reality. He could hear the Target employee freaking out. "Oh my gosh. Oh, that is so disgusting. I'm not cleaning it. Holy mother, it's on the ceiling!"

At this point Michael is faced with yet another two choices.

Choice one: he could own the situation and apologize and try to make it right (this would not be a man I could marry).

Choice two: he could become my future husband and pass the blame on someone else.

Like a man truly worthy of marriage, he responded to the young employee by saying. "Yeah, man, that's disgusting. Someone should clean that up." He zipped up the pants, washed his hands, and strolled out of that Target like nothing happened.

It was at this exact moment, when Michael finished sharing that amazingly real, horrible experience with me, that I knew I could marry him. Because he was willing to reveal the real him. Because that story was *bad*, and he still told it to me. And not only did Michael tell it to me, he now lets me tell the entire world because he knows that a story can actually do something great. If this story can sell me on marriage, I know your stories can sell the product or service that is resting in your soul and won't let you go.

So let's talk about stories. I want to help you connect what we know about being authentic and what we know about why people buy products. I want to make it abundantly clear to you that the way to get people to buy into your business is by being who you are and telling real, authentic stories about yourself and about the product or services you are offering.

The Five Parts of a Good Story

For centuries we've known that a good story has been made up of the same five components. Originally identified by the ancient Greek philosopher and scientist Aristotle, these components have stood the test of time. Great storytellers throughout history, from Homer to Shakespeare to J.K. Rowling, have created amazing works of art by employing these five simple components in the right order:

1. **Exposition:** The opening of the story, where the storyteller introduces some characters and a conflict sets the stage for what's about to happen.
2. **Rising Action:** This is where the character(s) meets the conflict.
3. **Climax:** Suspense and emotion build as the character(s) takes action to resolve the conflict.
4. **Falling Action:** Have you noticed how short a story usually is once the climax is reached? I have often thought, *How is this author going to end this book with only two pages left?* That's because the rising action and the climax make up the bulk of the story. The falling action is just not as exciting and can usually be summed up in fewer words than the rising action. It consists of the events that lead to final resolution of the conflict.
5. **Resolution:** Here the storyteller ties everything up with a bow for the audience.

In diagram form, the story components look like this:

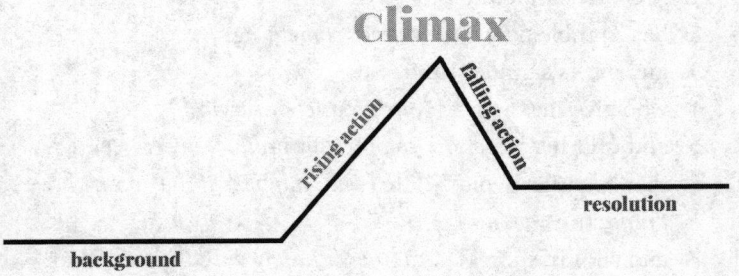

When I invest my time in watching a movie, and one of these components is missing in the storytelling, I can always tell. It's that feeling you get walking out of the theater that the story wasn't quite finished, that something was missing or the story just wasn't as satisfying as you thought it could have been. I find this especially true when the movie doesn't have a strong resolution. when there's been all this build-up, and then there's nothing to help me tie it all together. I don't want to have to make up the ending. I want the storyteller to give it to me.

Remember that. Your audience wants you to wrap everything up for them in a perfect little package and then tell them what to do next. As you use stories to tell customers about your business, do this for them, and don't be afraid to ask for what you want at the end.

I would be remiss if I didn't reference Donald Miller when I talk about storytelling. Miller is the author of amazing books, such as *Scary Close*[1] and *Building a StoryBrand*[2] and is one of my favorite online mentors who has no idea who I am. He has studied the art of storytelling as it applies to marketing and has come up with what he calls a BrandScript, where he basically follows the five components of great storytelling but adds a few pieces to help clarify the message so the audience doesn't end up confused about what the storyteller is trying to communicate. He also shows how all effective marketing itself is basically a form of storytelling.

The steps to his BrandScript (which he says almost every good movie also follows) can be summed up in a single sentence (I've added some parenthetical comments to show how this can apply to storytelling in your business):

1. A character (*your customer*)
2. has a problem (*wants or needs something*)
3. and meets a guide (*you!*)
4. who gives her a plan (*your product or service*)
5. and calls her to action (*to buy your product or service*)
6. that helps her avoid failure (*what happens if she doesn't have your product*)
7. and ends in success (*customer is happy with the purchase*).[3]

Miller references epic films series, such as *Harry Potter*, *Star Wars*, and *The Hunger Games*, and even fun movies, like *Tommy Boy*, to show how closely most good stories conform to this pattern.

I want you to get comfortable with this idea of storytelling as a marketing tool, both online and in person. That means that at times you'll be writing out your stories and at times you'll be presenting them live. Start by working on telling a story in a casual way when you're interacting with friends and see how they react. Do they laugh where you're expecting it? What are their follow-up questions like? It doesn't have to always be about your product. Find ways to weave stories into anything you're talking about rather than rattling off facts and figures.

How to Explode Your Brain

If you've been alive in the last ten years, you've probably heard of TED Talks. And if you've watched even one of them online, you've likely seen Simon Sinek's talk on starting with why—it's called "How Great Leaders Inspire Action."[4] While the production quality isn't great, the subject matter blew my mind when I first heard it. It's been translated into forty-seven different languages and has been viewed nearly forty million times on the TED website alone. Sinek wrote a book about the same topic called *Start with Why*,[5] which I highly recommend. Both the TED Talk and the book explain why companies that sell their stories of *why* they do what they do have more success than those that simply talk about what they do.

Here's some great news: our brains don't distinguish much between hearing a story of an event and actually experiencing it. That's why we can get so engrossed in a Netflix series. We may even stay up seven days binge watching our new favorite show.* We get invested in these shows, and we feel a need to know what is going to happen. We get a little buzz

....

* Ahem, *Game of Thrones*, ahem.

from the stories we hear, and that activity actually shows up in brains scans.*

Did you know our brains actually release dopamine into our system to make us feel good and crave more when we listen to an emotionally charged story? That very same chemical creates a situation where we remember more with greater accuracy. That explains the Netflix bingeing phenomenon. It's also why we put ourselves through a day of torture after we get hooked into a new book and can't put it down until four in the morning. It's why I have very real nightmares about whatever scary thing I've just seen on TV or read in the paper. That story becomes my life—so much so that I start to associate all the bad things that are happening around the world or on that show to actually happening to me or the people I love.

Let's talk a little more about the human brain for a second. There are three main parts to our brain: the rational part, the emotional part, and the instinctive part. If a salesperson starts rattling off facts about what their product can do for you, your rational brain will kick in and process that information—but that's not the part of the brain where decisions on buying are made. So after you're presented with a bullet-point list of features and benefits, you have to access a totally different part of your brain to make a buying decision.

Now, let's assume that after the facts and figures, that same salesperson describes the solution to your problems or paints a verbal picture of the value of the product to your life. Your emotional brain will wake up and process the ways that information can meet an emotional need for you. You're getting closer to saying yes at this point. But this still isn't where the buying decision is made.

Buying decisions are made in the instinctual part of the brain. When someone describes a situation to you in the form of a story, it's the instinctual part of the brain that gets triggered. You start imagining that story inside your brain and it becomes real to you—it becomes an experience. When we hear a story, we start automatically linking these stories to our

....

* So, yes, Netflix, I *would* like to watch the next episode, and I'll thank you to stop judging me after every single one. Just keep it rolling—no need to ask again. Bye.

own experiences, making them even more real for us, personally. Stories are what tie our emotions to the product being sold. This process is called neural coupling.

Our brains explode with activity both when we're telling and hearing a compelling story. If you were to watch the brain activity in a person telling the story and that of the audience, you'd see the same parts of their brains begin to buzz with activity during the story. This is a process called mirroring. You can imagine that when someone tells you a story associated with a product they're passionate about, the product will become more personal to you too. The same areas of your brain start to light up, and you're much more likely to buy that product.[6]

Our emotions begin to take over the buying process when they're stimulated correctly, and our emotional reactions happen in less than three seconds. Seriously, it's that quick. According to Dan Hill, author of *Emotionomics: Leveraging Emotions for Business Success*, that's one-fifth the time it takes our rational brain to process the same input. And not only is the emotional/instinctive response quicker, but "our emotional reaction to a stimulus [such as a story] resounds more loudly in our brain than does our rational response, triggering the action to follow."[7]

Here's the bottom line: people don't buy products. Instead, they buy feelings, emotions, people, and stories. Your customer will press Buy because her gut tells her she can trust you. And she will trust you because she feels that you and her are basically alike. So there's no faster way to get to that place with your customer than to tell her your stories.

The Truth About Imperfection

As your business starts to grow, you may start to notice that your customers and followers put you on a pedestal. They will lift you up as someone to be emulated and followed, which you are, especially if you've built your brand on authenticity. Often they'll start to believe that your life is a version of perfect that they wish they had. They'll start to expect perfection from you even though you know there's no such thing.

It makes sense then that you may be afraid of getting honest. If you tell stories that reveal you're not so perfect, will it affect the way your customer sees you? The answer is yes. Telling real stories *will* change the way customers see you. You will destroy the perfect image that people have wrongly assume about you. You will let them see that you're just like them. You have problems just as they do. You'll give them the chance to connect to the ways you're alike rather than to the ways you're different.

Our imperfections are what bind us together. They allow your customers and those in your tribe to take you off of the pedestal and put you in the seat right next to them—where they have the ability to feel like your equal—where they can be honest with you about their felt needs. When you show your imperfections, you get the chance to build an honest relationship with your customers.

My friend Melissa is an extremely successful and amazing entrepreneur. But for the longest time she let the fact that she doesn't have a college degree hold her back from stepping into the role of strong female leader—a role she had already earned yet had not owned. At one point, however, Melissa decided to be brave and share this "secret shame" with her customers and followers. She created a social media post about the very thing that was holding her back and told her people how she felt about not getting that secondary education.

I wish you could have seen the response Melissa got from that raw and autentic post about her insecurity. She received not only messages of support, but also lots of "me too" messages.

You guys, she built a tribe that day, a tribe of like-minded people. And she didn't sacrifice her place in her business because she spoke honestly about something that was difficult for her to overcome. That acceptance from her tribe allowed her to step into her role as leader in the entrepreneurship field!

That makes sense when you think about it. Ask yourself, *Would someone being honest about their insecurities make me feel more connected to them or turned off by their imperfection?*

It's hard, though, because when we're the one who has to go first, we worry that people will turn from us because of our truth. But the opposite is true.

So say the thing that matters. Tell people about what troubles you. Express your excitement about your life and your business. Talk about the imperfections. Speak your truth and let the people who can't handle it go.

Dare to tell your stories—all of them.

7

SUCCESS PHILOSOPHY #4:
BRAND CONSISTENCY MATTERS

As we discussed in chapter 4, your brand is not just your logo, colors, fonts, and icons. Your brand is so much more. It's the way you talk, the images you take, the feel of your social-media posts, the way you present yourself in public, your message, your theme, the people you target, the content you create.

Your brand, in other words, is everything you do. It's your entire online and in-person presence.

The great news is that you get to decide the kind of brand you want to create around your business. Part of that process is thinking through all the things we talked about in chapter 4, when we laid the foundation for your business. But another important part is creating content and messaging that is consistent to that brand. The more off-brand you go, the more confused your audience will become—and guys, confusion kills.

Make sure your message is consistent and represents you. This includes any time you're representing your brand. Consistency is a critical part in the trust-building that you will need to have between your brand (you) and your customer.

Understanding Your Audience

My first business that really took off for me was my essential oils business. What I noticed when I fell in love with the product was that the current market for it largely consisted of people who were outside of my target customer. I wanted to reach young moms between the ages of twenty-five and forty. But it became quickly and abundantly clear to me that the standard marketing and branding for these products were such a turnoff to people in my chosen market (read: people like me) that my target customers wouldn't even consider those tiny little bottles of awesome. I didn't want to be responsible for that misconception. I knew that if I was going to serve my customers the right way, I would have to take responsibility for reaching them in a different way.

My business was born out of a vision to bring essential oils to a younger market than was currently being catered to. This market cares a lot about what the things they purchase look like, which is especially true if they're going to be spending a good chunk of their money on it. So I did a lot of thinking about packaging. I wanted to offer something young, fresh, clean, bright, and cute.

I also wanted to make it clear that oils weren't just for forty-five-to-sixty-year-old women or the tofu and granola natural-foods crowd. That's where most of the essential-oils marketing seemed to be aimed at the time. I wanted to show that oils can be for anyone at any level of commitment to a natural lifestyle. In reaching my customers, I wanted to create a home for people who hadn't gone all-in on everything health and wellness yet, a place for the misfits in the barrage of information and products that is the health and wellness industry.

I myself am part-time crunchy granola and part-time Chick-fil-A,* and I knew a lot of women like me. So I decided my target market and my team would be largely made up of people who love their oils and use them but also aren't afraid to stop for a Happy Meal if it had been one of those

---

* #1, no pickles, with sweet tea.

days with the kids. I wanted to make sure our brand represented that. I wanted it to say, "Oils don't have to be weird. Trust us. We use them too, and we're just like you."

Once I understood who I was trying to reach, I immediately saw a need for better marketing, educational materials, and customer service, so I set out to rectify that for my people by offering exactly that. Understanding my audience and what they were looking for in a brand made all the difference in my business. Even without having control of what the product packaging looked like, I was able to connect with my customer by changing what I did have control over.

Was it difficult? Yes. Did it take a lot of hours? Yes. Did I have to invest my time and money into it? Yes. A lot of hours, issues, frustration—plus a lot of money from my paycheck that went back into my businesses.

Did it work? Absolutely.

I will continue to work my hardest to fill holes in the market and meet the needs of the people I serve so they can succeed faster and with more ease. I make it a priority to find ways to solve issues that don't involve depending on others; I believe it's up to me to create wins for both my teams and myself. Personally, I rely on God to do the rest. You can do that too. Be original, think outside the box, and go get what you want—just do it consistently.

Target Your Marketing to Your Target Market

One thing I see a lot of women who are trying to sell product do is basically throw up all over their social media feeds with information about their products, no matter who made it or compiled the info or what it looks like. That desperation is felt by potential customers, and it feels both manipulative and inauthentic. Hammering potential customers over the head with information from all over the World Wide Web sends the message that "I'm just looking for sales," not "I'm sharing information to help people."

I don't share *any* marketing pieces for my businesses if they aren't consistent to my brand. If I shared everything I see, it would confuse my potential customer. It's important to me that I keep things consistent and clean in the way I communicate and the way my brand looks. I absolutely don't want people to get the impression that I'm desperate for sales.

Make sure you think about your target market each time you're about to put out information about the product or service you are selling. My business started with a post on Instagram to help moms, and I haven't wavered from that. Don't worry about what everyone else is doing. Instead, be conscious about how your brand is perceived by your potential customers.

If you're targeting a new market, consistency of approach is especially important. The net you cast shouldn't be all-encompassing. It's really okay and definitely smarter to find a niche market and meet the needs of those specific people. Become an expert on your target market, and you'll have a huge advantage.

I often see people fishing for every kind of person, and the things they post and talk about make me feel like they're just casting a line randomly into every pond, hoping to catch something. Customers sense that and steer clear. Our businesses can't successfully be all things to all people, and when we try, we're likely to alienate the very customers we want to reach.

My friend Elizabeth and I are alike in a lot of ways. She often knows what I'm thinking before I say it. She and I share a love for a lot of color, good music, food, and cute Internet animal videos. We laugh about the dumbest things together, and we've been coworkers now for the past four years. One thing we do not have in common is that Elizabeth is not a mom, which is one of the biggest parts of my life. She has no plans to be a mother, and I commend her for making the choice that is right for her. Liz isn't in my target market and I don't intentionally create content for people without kids. Liz is an outlier for me. She bought product from me despite the fact that I don't specifically market to her.

Just because I serve moms and talk a lot about my own parenting journey doesn't mean I won't pull in outliers like Elizabeth. In fact, I polled my followers last year and found that 30 percent of them do not have kids. Does that mean I abandon talking to moms? No. It simply proves that you and I can affect people outside our target markets with our brands even while keeping our marketing consistently focused on our target markets. It's great to get outliers, but stay consistent in who you're serving. Let the people who want to be a part of your tribe stay, and don't worry about the others.

Market *You* More Than Your Product

Part of being brand consistent is making sure the brand of you doesn't get taken over by your product or service. When you're starting out (before you have a slew of amazing employees and your business starts generating millions), it's so important that you as a person connect directly with your potential customers. That means you must put yourself into your conversations and social media posts as much (read: more) as you put your product.

I realize this might sound counterproductive. "Lindsay, if I want people to know I have a product to sell, don't I have to talk about it all the time?" I wish it was that simple, y'all. If only we lived in a world where we could just mention what we have to sell and people would fall all over themselves to book us or buy from us. But we don't.

It's one thing for a company that's well-established and has insane brand recognition to talk about their product all the time. It's quite another for a small business to do the same. We have to give our potential customers time to get to know us and our product, time to like us, time to trust us, and time to decide whether our product or service will meet their needs. That means that doing social media is going to be harder for us than it is for a company like Coke or Starbucks.

It's my firm belief that you as a small business owner don't have the luxury to just advertise your product on your feed. To get the best results, you have to ease your customer into the sale by letting them get to know both you and your product—but especially you. The winning combination I found while I was building my own business was to post once about my product and what I do and then post another four times on my feed about other things. The other posts could be industry-related information, little tips and tricks, insights into my personal life, behind-the-scenes posts, funny posts, or entertaining or educational reads. But they couldn't be a hard sell for my product or service.

Our customers aren't stupid. They know how to block out content that isn't going to relate to them. When our customers get used to seeing the same exact post worded in 174 different ways over and over again in our social media feeds, they condition themselves to scroll right past what we're saying.

Sister, our brains are capable of making twenty quadrillion (yea, that's totally a number) calculations in a single second. Making the decision to scroll past content that isn't going to entertain, teach, help, or excite us is so easy, we often don't even realize when we've made the choice. It happens without even having to think about it because we are amazing creatures with super computers for brains.

With that reality in mind, it's your job to keep your customers on their toes and create a desire in them to make sure they don't miss a post from you. Do that by mixing up your content and making sure you're spending enough time on that part of your business. Talk about your product, of course, but do it in that one-to-five ratio above. Make them fall in love with you, and they'll fall in love with the things you love—like your product or service. People will want to work with you, and you won't have to sell them if they feel like they know you. They'll know the person they're working with, and that is how you get repeat customers who tell their friends about you.

Delete Your Share Button

I see it all the time. One photographer or artist does something that creates some momentum in her business, and before you know it, every other photographer and artist is doing the same thing to try to recreate the buzz. When social media fads happen, the only way a consumer can get away from it is to scroll past the posts or unfollow the poster. I'm sure we can all think of multiple examples of this from our own social media feeds, often from people who sell a product through network marketing. I often think, *I've seen this before*, only to scroll through my feed and see the same post seventeen other times from people representing the same product.

Copying, pasting, and sharing are easier than creating your own original content, of course, and it can easily become your default. But using other's stuff (even really good stuff) is not going to help you stand out from the competition, and your customer will only hang around for so much of it. Your voice is missing when you don't take the time to write your own content. And your tribe needs your voice.

Let's explore how customers might feel if they see multiple social media posts that are simply copied and pasted and perhaps just like those from your competition.

Reaction #1: "I Feel Sold To"

The first thing I feel when I keep seeing the same thing popping up in my news feed from different people is "sold to.' I start to wonder if the post is intended to actually help and engage me or just to get my money. And I think your customers probably feel that way too.

When people choose to buy a product from you, it's because they trust you to connect what they need with what you have. They're trusting that your product or service will work for them like you said it would. And they like to feel that you see them as something more than a source of income. But when they see a big group of people all posting the same thing, if the words aren't yours, then the natural assumption is that they're being sold something, and when a product needs to be sold like that, there's a good chance it's not that great. The trust starts to go backward and not forward.

Reaction #2: "I Can't Hear You!"

In addition, as people get used to your posts sneaking into their social media feeds or they read or watch your video stories, they'll become accustomed to your tone and the way you communicate. They'll start to "hear" you speaking through your written posts as well and be more likely to read them. But when you copy and paste someone else's writing, that connection you have with your customers is missing.

Let your online customers relate to the way you talk, the way you position your words, the slang you use. As you write original content, imagine your target customer sitting in front of you, poised to hear what you have to say today. Write to that one person, but—this is important—do it the way you speak.

This might be a challenge, especially if you were born before 1985, if you grew up before texts and social media, or if you had a really good (or really opinionated) English teacher. I often see people get onto their social media feed and write what sounds like a formal letter instead of natural speech.

Writing like you speak probably isn't what your teacher taught you in school, but's it's the right way to communicate on social media. Slang and text abbreviations are fine. Contractions are great. Sentence fragments and emoticons are preferred. The only thing that really matters is developing a consistent and recognizable voice. The better you get at maintaining it online, the easier it will be for you to remain brand consistent. The way you speak and write are a part of your brand.

PRO TIP

Here's an excellent way to practice the art of writing like you speak. You'll need pencil and paper, a cellphone, and a good friend you're comfortable talking to.

First, pick one of the questions below—whichever would be easiest for you to answer—and write out the answer as if you were going to post it on social media. (This should take about two minutes.)

- Question 1: What do you wish you did more often?
- Question 2: If life ended today, what would you regret not doing?
- Question 3: What habit would you most like to start/stop?

Now set your answer aside and grab your phone and your friend. (You can do this over Skype, Zoom, or FaceTime if your friend isn't with you in person.)

Have your friend hold your phone, open the voice memo app, and start recording, then take about a minute to answer the same question out loud. Look at your friend and talk to her normally, the way you would if she'd asked you the question.

When the recording is finished, transcribe your voice memo onto a different piece of paper so you can see the exact words you used and how the information flowed when you spoke the answer rather than wrote it. Then compare your two answers. How are they similar? How are they different? How might you be able to practice writing more like you speak so your audience can hear your voice as they read your words? You can always keep transcribing your spoken words into written words, if needed, until it becomes easier.

Reaction #3: "I've Seen That One Before"

So if you're reposting others' pictures, your audience will remember, and your credibility will go out the window because they'll know you're not using genuine content. Take the time to get yourself a subscription to a really great stock photo library or learn how to take eye-catching images of your product and your life for your customers to see. Great images compel your audience to take the time to read what you've written—but they need to be original.

Reaction #4: "What's the Story?"

When you share posts from others, instead of your own, your audience misses the story—your story—that connects her, the customer, to you, the salesperson. Remember, we are hardwired to connect through story. Facts and figures only go so far to actually get people to buy the product. Your customers need your story. They need your experience. They need *you*.

Again, there's a simple remedy to these four potential responses. Simple, but not easy.

Take the time to create your own content.[*]

Be inspired by how other people present information. Let their ideas help you create ones of your own. But come up with your own materials so your customers have the benefit of your voice, your brand, your point of view.

Your social media posts should be a big part of your job. You should be spending time on them to make your posts unique and on-brand. Don't let what's easy take you on a shortcut to nowhere.

....
* I know. I'm blowing your mind. Best money you've ever spent on a book.

SUCCESS PHILOSOPHY #5: USE THE UNSALES TACTIC

For some reason many of us are under the impression that to be a good salesperson we have to understand everything about how to trick a customer into buying from us. I once had someone give me a sales pitch for a product, and it was one of the most awkward conversations I've ever had because the words coming out of my friend's mouth were completely foreign. I asked why she was talking so strangely. And she said that she'd been to a sales training and it was best for her to use a script to talk to potential clients rather than simply having a conversation. "It just works better," she told me, parroting what she had been taught.

Well, maybe it does work better for some (though I cannot imagine who). But I had zero desire to buy her product because she'd spent approximately zero time being someone I could trust with my money and resources. At that exact moment I knew that one day I'd write this exact chapter of this exact book—because while sales is indeed a skill, it isn't the part of your job where you completely abandon everything that makes you who you are and become some kind of sales robot.

Selling is a skill that you can learn. There's a right way and a wrong way to convince a customer to purchase your product or service. But the right way is not what a lot of people imagine. For some reason, many are under the impression that being a good salesperson means tricking customers into buying. But that's the very opposite of what I believe is the most effective approach.

What's my alternative? I call it the unsales tactic. It's a strategic plan in which you reject the way you've been told to sell a product and instead start doing what is best for your customer—even if it's not the right time for them to purchase from you. The unsales tactic explores your customers' needs, understands the things that may be holding them back from buying, builds trust, and sets your business apart from your competition.

Revolutionary, right? Here's how it works.

Exploring Your Customers' Needs

The first step to learning the unsales tactic is exploring your customers' needs.

Think about education or health. Everybody already knows these things are good for them. They just need to figure out how they work in their lives right now and how this product or service could affect them. The first step is to determine their need by asking them. Get in a conversation about their pain point. There has to be value for them right now, so your first job is to find out more about them so you can show that value.

For example, we know we need to be drinking a buttload of water every single day.* If I were selling an app that helps owners track the water they should be drinking and gives great reminders, I'd begin by getting some idea of my customer's felt needs (by asking questions).

Second, I would offer some understanding about how they may feel about those needs. "I know. I hear you. We all need to drink more water, and that's probably the most boring and uninspiring thing ever, right? I often can't remember if I even ate breakfast, let alone drank water." This

---

* I'm pretty sure it's 283 gallons of water we should be consuming every day. I consume .6 gallons, and it's usually in the form of sweet tea. Just saying.

is a perfect spot to lead into a short story about how you've been in their shoes.

Next, I would move to the reason this app will be different, why it stands out from other apps, and how it will add value to their life. "I have this app on my phone that reminds me every so often with a notification to chug eight ounces and move on with my day. The notifications are hilarious, and you can play games as you chug alone or with fellow water drinkers. This app makes drinking water actually fun and easy to remember."

And then I end with the call to action: "Just try it. This app has changed the way I remember to do this simple task and has already created a new habit for me. Here's the link."

When it comes to your product or service, you have to connect the dots between your customers' needs and what you have to give. Don't bombard them with facts and figures. Don't overpromise them anything. If you're truly in touch with your customers' needs, then your days will be consumed with how you can meet those needs.

When Michael brings me coffee to try to coax me out of bed in the morning, I'm usually on my phone, scrolling through the places where I interact with my tribe.* I see what they're saying. I read their comments. I take note of the customers' tone, and I figure out how I can bring value to them today. What can I do that I don't see other businesses doing right now? How can I make them feel?

Honestly, this kind of intentional work at paying attention to my customers and audience takes diligence and focus. But it's so important to understanding both their existing and evolving needs and figuring out the best ways to meet them.**

Another way of looking at your customers' needs—or felt needs—is through identifying their pain points. Now, when we talk about pain in this context, we're not talking about advanced cancer or a spontaneous

....

* That's a lie. I'm usually asleep because I am the absolute worst version of myself before eight in the morning. Coffee makes me tolerable, so really Michael is just protecting himself. Well played, husband.
** Bonus: I also find this is where new product ideas usually come from.

amputation. We're talking about the little (or not-so-little) disappointments and discomforts that might prompt a customer to seek relief. Some pain points are physical, and some are simply inconveniences we deal with throughout our lives.

Mark Suster wrote in *Inc.* magazine:

> Pain is a reminder that unless your prospect has a need to solve a problem, they are not going to buy a product. Customers sometimes buy things spontaneously without thinking through what they actually need. But, often, there is an underlying reason for a purchase, even if the buyer doesn't bring it to the surface.[1]

Let's say you've spent the time observing your customers on social media or wherever you interact with them, just as I do each morning. You've identified a customer's pain point because you're in touch with how she's feeling and what's going on with her. How, then, do you connect the dots between her pain point and what you have to give?

Let's start with what not to do: stop making it all about you.

I see this a lot on social media, and it's not nearly as effective as people think it is. Telling your story is great, but just saying "I love this product" doesn't necessarily attract people.* Your social media posts, blog posts, and conversations about your product have to have a point, and the object of every one should be to connect through a common need or pain point. Your pain is their pain, and if that's honestly true, you get them. If you're selling something, what you say cannot be about you; it needs to be about your customer. Don't be a crocodile (really big mouth and really small ears).[2]

Example: "I'm totally digging this new recipe book." What does this mean to your people? Where's the pain point? You just wasted your opportunity to connect!

I see this kind of thing a lot when it comes to the whole work thing. Posts like "look how hard I work, *I* need this product too"—which on the surface seem to be about storytelling and sharing but are really just pats

....

* You're just saying something to hear yourself talk at that point.

on our own backs under the pretense of touching a pain point. That's fake, and customers don't relate to fake.

In the case of the recipe book, what should have been said is something like this:

> You guys, I've been on the struggle bus for the last couple of years, and based on my social media feed, I know I'm not alone. Why is getting fat so fun and easy and losing it such a shame-fueled struggle? Anybody else feel me?
>
> As my body gets older I'm noticing a real difference in how hard it has been to lose weight and stay healthy. To be honest, there are a lot of days when I downright hate the way I look in the mirror—so much so that I sometimes avoid doing it. I avoid jumping into the pool with my kids too. I find myself shying away from going to see people who may notice that my weight isn't what it used to be.
>
> At the same time, I know this diet culture isn't good for me, and I find myself wondering what I should be eating. It's confusing and depressing and, honestly, I think it's just what the health industry wants. The more confused I am, the more likely I am to buy all the things they want to sell me.
>
> I've decided to give this new recipe book a try to see what a consistent, healthy diet will do for me. I've loved the recipes I've tried from it so far, and the meals haven't been expensive or confusing. No counting calories or carbs, and no keeping track of points either. I need easy, and I need yummy when it comes to eating, you know, and so far that's what I've found in this book. I hope you'll give this a try with me and see what this could do for your health. My Facebook group is open for you to be a part of the community, and I'd love to have you join me. I may even throw in a few workouts during the week . . . maybe!

Does a post like this take more time?

Yep.

Does it touch on your pain point and the customers' too?

Yep.

Is it about the potential customer instead of me?

Yep. This is a little subtle though. I do talk about myself and my issues, but I specifically relate that to what the customer may be feeling.

The difference is still clear. The first example is just a regurgitation. It's the tell-and-sell tactic. All you're doing is going through the same motions hoping you can tell your people what to do in order to sell to them, when what you need to do is listen more and then speak to what you hear.

Take the time to make it about the reader. Don't be a crocodile.

The best way to stop making it all about you is to have a conversation with your customers as they ask you questions about your product or service. After all, it's natural for them to want to know more before impulsively pressing Buy on what it is you're selling. So the more you can engage in conversations with them, the more you'll learn what they need and how you can meet those needs.

You might need to guide the conversation a little to get to the need. Most likely someone will say something neutral, like, "Tell me more about this," or "I need that too." You can tease out pain points from that conversation:

1. Connect over what initially brought them to talk to you.
2. Let them know what you do. Tell them very briefly—I mean it, briefly—your unique selling proposition. Something like, "So look, I'm building a community of women who are trying to get their health under control while also doing all of the things most women do during the day. We'll talk about everything from tips and tricks to recipes and fun workouts. It's a no-judgment kind of group, different than anything I've seen on the Internet." Resist the urge to vomit out information, especially if you're writing it out. People don't care much about facts and figures or lots of text.
3. Ask open-ended questions that you're genuinely curious about as it pertains to what the potential customer is dealing with and the product you sell. Get really good at the art of asking people good questions to get to know them. I personally find this easier to practice in written conversations than when I'm on the spot in person, but either way it's a learned skill. Cultivate and practice it. Let your

people tell their stories to you. Connect with them. They need to know you get them. In the above example about community building, you're creating a support place for them that could eventually lead to being able to sell them the product you have connected to that need.

4. If you can, let them know they're not the first customer you've had who has had this issue. Normalize their pain point. This is especially true if they are having difficulty telling you about it.

5. If appropriate, transition into the sale by using phrases like "What I've found . . ." "What I've found is that moms are prone to sitting in their houses and hiding the stress and the mess that comes along with just being a mom. There's not enough time for all the healthy meals you know you should be creating, and it's just easier to grab something quick from a drive-through. I know that's true for me. That's where a community of people can come in and at least make the process of creating healthy meals a little less painful. Know what I mean?"

6. Connect the product directly to their issue. You be the judge of how to do that on the basis of your interaction with them. Let them talk, joke with them, or empathize with them, whatever seems appropriate. Just be you, and make sure you show them how what you have to offer can meet the need they've just told you they have.

Remember to resist the urge to talk over your customers, even on social media. Just let them talk to you. Make your own communications brief and to the point. Your customers are human beings who want their pain, their needs, to be understood. If they don't know why they're inquiring about your product, it's up to you to figure out how best to help them by asking good questions. I guarantee, there is a reason.

Every human in the world has pain points. When it comes to buying anything, there's an opportunity cost, and there most likely needs to be a reason for people to press Buy or to subscribe to what it is you're selling—even if the reason is just an online community or a mailing list. Once you get your customers to open up to you about their pain points, you're well on your way to helping them solve their problems.

Understanding What May Be Holding Your Customers Back

A few years ago Michael and I took the girls to dinner at Mimi's Cafe. At the table across from us sat a woman, who looked to be in her forties, with a man I assumed was her husband. They seemed to be at the restaurant for a serious reason. There wasn't a lot of talking at that table, and you could feel the tension between the two.

On the other side of us was a cute little family with a toddler. And about halfway through the meal, we heard the unmistakable sound of that toddler standing up under the table and slamming the top of her head into the corner of it.

That sound was directly followed by ten entire seconds of silence, which every parent knows was the sound of a child summoning all of the energy of the universe before letting 'er rip. This kid won the screaming Olympics on this day and rightfully so. She'd hit that table with the force of an NFL linebacker.

Within four seconds of the wailing, the woman across from us yelled out for everyone in the entire restaurant to hear. "Hey lady, would you shut that kid up!"

Oooooooh no, she did not, I said to myself as my blood turned hot and I prepared for a fight.

Yes, she did.

My head snapped over to her table, and my mouth fell open. I'm pretty sure I saw a woman over in the corner start to sharpen her spoon into a shiv. *That's right, lady. We got this.*

Everyone I could see in that restaurant was looking back and forth from the table with the crying kid to the woman who had just yelled. I wasn't sure where this was going to go, but I was angry for that other mom. I know what it feels like to have a kid screaming and know there's nothing you can do to make it better.

At this point I looked over at Michael, who was looking empathetically toward the woman who had just lashed out. *He's feeling bad for her? Why? She was horrible.*

Then, before I knew it, the woman began to weep. She covered her face, got up from the table, and ran toward the front doors of the restaurant. And do you know what her husband did? He acted like nothing had happened. He continued to eat his dinner and even asked the waitress for a drink refill. Michael and I just sat there, confused. You guys, that husband didn't even look up to see if his wife had left the building.

As the little one who smacked her head on the table began to calm down, we finished our dinner, and I began to realize I should have had more empathy for the woman who screamed. Michael knew it right away. Something just wasn't right there. We have no idea what she was going through. Maybe they were going through a divorce. Maybe they had been dealing with a tragedy. I just don't know. But there was definitely something wrong, and I definitely should have felt for her. In hindsight, it would take a lot of stress and heartbreak for me to lash out like that. If it were me, I would probably want someone to have some empathy for my situation.

The Case for Empathy

It is so easy to make snap judgments about a situation without having all the details. I've decided that we should just make the blanket assumption that everyone is doing the best they can in a given moment. We should automatically give them grace and strive for empathy, which Merriam-Webster's Eleventh Collegiate Dictionary Edition defines as

> the action of understanding, being aware of, being sensitive to, and vicariously experiencing the feelings, thoughts, and experience of another of either the past or present without having the feelings, thoughts, and experience fully communicated in an objectively explicit manner.

I have to admit, though, that empathy is a learned skill for me. I didn't come preprogrammed with a lot of empathy for the feelings of others, and I have a lot of my hard-edge, get-it-done-and-don't-make-excuses attitude to blame for that. To be perfectly honest, I wasn't raised with a whole lot of empathy, either. Learning it has been a difficult and important struggle for me.*

The church I currently belong to does a pretty good job of being an example of empathy. One of their founding principles is the "me too" idea. There isn't any standing up on the stage and condemning the congregation for their sins. Instead, our church strives to create an environment where people can "bump into Jesus" and let God handle the rest.

There's a lot of "We get you; you're not the only one struggling" going on at that church, which makes it a great place to belong because you don't have to pretend to be perfect. I can imagine that to the church leaders (who are imperfect humans, of course), it feels good to know they don't have to play that perfect pastor role for their community of people.

Our church is a great example of the empathy that needs to be part of your unsales strategy too. You should find ways to let the people you interact with know you understand their situation and care about it. Instead of treating the pain points they're giving you as sales tools, you stop and take the time to understand how they may be feeling,

Practicing empathy for people's situations helps you know the right course of action in your business too. If you've really paid attention, you probably have a sense whether they're ready, even eager, to say yes to you and your product or service. You know if they truly cannot afford the product at this time or if that's an excuse. If it's something they really need but cannot buy, perhaps you can set them up with a plan to afford it in the future. You can even admit that now might not be the right time for them to buy. In my experience this small, empathetic response to money issues goes a long way to create trust—and to be honest, it's just the right thing to do.

It might feel counterintuitive, of course, to voluntarily give up a sale. But you'd better believe that a customer will remember if you put their needs in front of your own when it comes to business, and they'll be back to buy if the value is there for them.

Can you imagine what it would feel like to have a leader, friend,

....

* I have my husband and Brené Brown to thank for any progress I've made here.

or business owner make you feel like you weren't alone in your pain? Wouldn't you want to be around that more? Wouldn't it create more brand loyalty in you? Wouldn't you do better at being a friend to that person?

Now imagine what developing honest (not fake or manipulative) empathy can do for your business. Get in the habit of really looking and listening and trying to figure out where your customers are coming from. What are their hang-ups? What is making them feel uneasy? Don't push people who have just told you something painful. Understand it and do what's best for them, and then you can decide whether your product or service can help them with that pain.

Working on your empathy skills and abilities will help every relationship and interaction you have. There's no downside to understanding and truly feeling with others. It will make you a better human being, and chances are it will also build more loyalty and trust from your potential customers.

How can you express empathy with your next customer? The good news is there isn't a right or wrong way. According to Brené Brown,

> Empathy has no script.
> There is no right or wrong way to do it.
> It's simply listening, holding space, withholding judgement, emotionally connecting, and communicating that incredibly healing message of "you're not alone."[3]

The Art of Active Listening

Beyond developing empathy, another step to understanding what may be holding your customers back is learning the art of active listening. The good news is that, like empathy, this is a skill you can learn and put into practice.* Active listening will help you in your personal relationships, but it's going to help you in business as well.

I hate to admit it, but much of the time when I should be listening,

....

* Even if it's difficult to learn, as in my case! It's one I still work on because I often fail miserably and don't even notice someone else's pain until the moment has passed.

I'm actually formulating a response in my head. Do you ever find your-self doing this same thing? I don't believe I'm unique in that regard. I believe most people listen first to respond instead of to understand the other person.

You know those people who always make you feel super important after you leave them? Like after you're done talking to them, you realize they've made you feel like the most important person in the room. Imagine if that was the kind of feeling that is associated with your brand. I find that the people who make me feel that way—like my Aunt Mary and my friend Rosy—are also the best active listeners. Their listening skills are off the charts, and when I am with them, those same listening skills let me know that I'm important to them. The least I can do is try to do the same for the people I interact with in my business and my personal life as well.

I once heard human behavior expert Vanessa Van Edwards talk about going to an event and taking a vow of silence to practice being a better listener. She held up a sign explaining what she was trying to do and then spent the rest of the event interacting with people. She said she was amazed at what people told her that evening without her responding ver-bally at all.

That's a great exercise but probably not practical in our daily interac-tions. There are still a number of practical steps that can help you hone your listening skills. Here are just a few:

1. *Turn and face the person who is talking to you.* Show her she has your full attention by putting away any communication devices (plus books, papers, magazines, and the like) and making eye contact. Don't creep the other person out by staring, but let her know her time is impor-tant to you and that you want to hear what she has to say.

Here's the part that I'm sure most of us wish we could just skim past because we've all done this, but "no communications devices" means put down the dang phone when someone is asking for your attention. Don't have it in your hands. Don't place it on the table (even upside down). Don't fiddle with it even without looking. Simply holding a phone tells others we are with that they aren't as important as whatever might come through on that phone. If you want people to feel like they're really being heard, make sure your phone is in your bag or in your back pocket—somewhere out of sight.

2. *Give the person talking your real attention.* Again, you don't have to be some robot who stares blankly into the other person's soul without blinking. That would be weird, and I'm sure it will scare people off. Be relaxed but attentive.

The most important part of this step is to continue paying attention. That's a challenge for me. Usually by about the third sentence of a conversation, I have started to make up in my head how the story will end and begin formulating my response.* I'm trying to break that habit because paying attention to the words people are using and actually letting those words work through your brain is so important to understanding the other person.

It's at this step that you're likely going to have to mentally block out the outside distractions—that baby who's crying, that dump truck out front, the relentless beeping coming from somewhere in the office, the kids screaming—they're all trying to get your attention. You'll have to deliberately ignore those sounds in order to remain present in your conversation. Make a note of the sound if you must—at least long enough to know if it represents an emergency. Then do your best to pull your attention back to the person talking to you.

3. *Listen without jumping to conclusions.* There are certain personality types that are going to struggle more with this than others. I'm talking to you, my outgoing talkers of the bunch. I'm one of those, friends, so you're not alone. If you're the guy that jumps to the "I know where this is going" and can't wait for the story to be over so we can get to the point, I get you—and we're wrong.

Practicing patience is critical to the art of listening. For a person like me who values powerful punches of information rather than a lot of detail, this can be tough, but it can be done, and it's the right thing to do. We have to let people communicate with us in their style and resist the urge

....

* What is actually wrong with me, you guys?

to jump to conclusions. This will help us understand our customers (and our friends and family) on a deeper level.

4. *Visualize what is being communicated to you.* You'll have a much easier time remembering and accessing the information you receive from listening if you can imagine the situation in your head along the way. This gives you a story to associate with that person. I promise it works.

5. *Resist the urge to provide solutions.* It's totally okay to ask people what they'd like from you or how you can help them during a conversation. But most of the time they will tell you they just need a listening ear—a place where they can hash out their thoughts and feelings. You may be able to see great solutions to the problems you're hearing—solutions are often easier to think of when you're not emotionally invested in the outcome. But it's important to reserve that information for when it's asked of you. Don't just jump in with unsolicited advice.

This is another one I struggle with because I'm a fixer. I will take care of problems using the fewest parts and following the fastest timeline, and this gives me some distinct advantages. But when I think about how my "fixing" must make others feel, I can see that it's also one of my most annoying attributes. It comes from a good place, sure, but that doesn't mean it's always the right thing to do.

6. *Ask clarifying questions.* Once there's a definite and purposeful pause in the conversation, you can now take the time to ask clarifying questions. "What did you mean when you said you're angry" or "How does this situation make you feel right now?" Those are clarifying questions.

What's not a clarifying question? "Oh, really? Let me tell you about a time this happened to me . . ." When we make others' stories all about us, it's clear we're not listening.

There are times when your personal stories can be both appropriate and helpful but only *after* you've really listened. Make sure you've given the other person time before you bring yourself into the mix.

7. *Give encouraging feedback.* It's important, especially if people are confiding in us or being vulnerable, to let them know we hear them

and are tracking with them. "Man, that is terrible, and I'm really sorry" or "I am so excited for you!" are great examples of how to give feedback without interrupting the other person's ability to finish.

8. *Know your nonverbal cues.* If someone is stepping back from you when they talk, give them more space. If they're telling you they're happy and their face says something different, work that into the conversation. If you sense boredom or sadness in someone else's nonverbal communication, don't discount those small cues. They could open up a great conversation between you and a person who might need you, client and friend alike. Take the cues and build understanding by asking more clarifying questions.

9. *Summarize.* This can be an awkward part of communication for me. It didn't flow very well when I first started doing it, but I've improved a lot since then. Simply repeating back to someone what they just said and asking for clarification can help a person feel heard and understood, and it also ensures that you're hearing them right. This is especially important when it comes to conflict resolution because misunderstood conversation can cause even more conflict. I use this summarizing technique with my girls a lot now. I ask how they're feeling, and after they tell me, I repeat what I heard back to them so they can correct or clarify with more detail if needed. It helps a lot, especially with my two anxious children.

How can these active listening techniques help with your sales (or unsales)? By making your customers feel heard, understood, and cared for. What better way to build trust?

Try these steps the next time you're having an interaction with a potential customer. Ask her about what is connecting them to your product or service. Let her tell you her story. Take it in fully and use your improved conversation skills to figure out how your products and services can actually fill a need and improve your customer's life.

If you can make her feel like the most important person in the room, she will feel great. On top of that, she will always have a special connection to your brand.

Setting Yourself Apart from Your Competition

This year Michael went on a trip to meet his Uncle Greg in New York City. The plan was to eat some good food, spend some quality time together, and watch both the Mets and the Yankees play. Both Michael and Greg are huge baseball fans, so Michael had really been looking forward to the trip. He had enough points to completely take care of a New York hotel room and was lucky enough to get a room at the Ritz-Carlton.

When he arrived at the hotel to check in, the guy at the front desk (Carlos) struck up a conversation with Michael about why he was in town. Michael mentioned the baseball games and how excited he was to see the two local teams play. Carlos checked Michael into his room and brought up his luggage, and Michael went out to meet Greg for a drink. When Michael returned to his room later that night, he found two brand new Yankees jerseys on the bed. Carlos had purchased two jerseys and gifted them to Michael and Greg for no other reason than to make Michael's trip more memorable.

How many companies would even work the ability for an employee to do that kind of thing into their budget? That's the kind of company you want to be loyal to, the kind of company you want to tell others about. Michael could have bought those jerseys for himself, but a giant hotel chain did it for him with no strings attached. That's customer service. That's what sets a business apart from its competition.

Standout Strategy #1: Outstanding Customer Service

The good news is that when it comes to customer service, these days the bar is low—like really low. It may be because I'm pushing forty—and complaining about customer service is a popular old person pastime—but there are few companies that wow me with service these days. Even the ones that used to build their reputation on service seem to have focused their efforts elsewhere.

What that means to you as an entrepreneur, of course, is that your business can really stand out by focusing on great customer service. You won't please everyone, of course, but a little effort in this area will go a long, long way. Focus on being responsive and proactive. Go the second mile, if you can, to make your customers happy and satisfied.

As you've already learned, people are going to emotionally connect to your brand. That means you're going to have to deal with those emotions as you build your business. As a provider of a product or service, you're bound to come across and work with a wide variety of people over the course of your career. But the emotional connections you'll establish with those people will mostly fall into one of two general categories. People will either have positive emotions about your brand and their experience with you, or they'll have negative emotions toward you. In other words, they'll either write you when they're really happy or they'll write to you when they're hacked off.

When customers are excited and positive about the product or service you've given them, you get to be excited about it too—that's what surprise and delight is all about. Let them tell you their story and what your brand has done for them. Match their level of excitement. Adapt to their communication style. These are the people you want to be part of your tribe, so joke around with them when it's appropriate. Let them see the human side of your brand, and you can turn them into "sticky" customers—those who not only buy your product repeatedly but who also talk about it to others, effectively becoming a brand ambassador for you. Customers will appreciate your taking the time to make them feel special when they've worked to do the same for you.

Negative customer interactions, of course, are much more challenging. When they come to you disappointed, angry, or frustrated, it's important to control your own emotions. I often puff up and feel the need to defend my brand when someone tears it down because I feel like they're really tearing me down. Believe me, it doesn't help! So take a step back if you feel your emotions starting to match the customers'. Be understanding and show compassion and empathy for them. When you respond to them in person or in writing, either let them know you understand their issue (if you do) or ask more questions so you can understand better and empathize with them. Reassure these customers that you're going to do your best to make them happy. Assure them you're working on the problem if one has been revealed to you.

People can go from zero to a hundred really fast over something that didn't live up to their expectations. I've had customers completely flip out on me and call me (and my staff) horrible names over such a scenario. But when they're worked up, we cannot be. All we can be is understanding and reassuring and do our best to remedy the issue.

There will always be a few customers that you cannot make happy for whatever reason. They didn't read the fine print or the instructions, the product isn't what they thought and you can't change it—it could be anything. And there are times when you have to let customers like that go. My mom used to call them "deletes." They are the customers who will never be ambassadors for your brand. Customers who are looking to take advantage of you. Customers who just cannot be satisfied. They're out there, and they will find you, I promise.

When this happens, it's important that you remember your values and your mission. Draw boundaries around what you will and will not do to make a customer happy, and then let the matter go. You cannot spend all of your time and resources trying to make the impossible happen. Don't be afraid to refund and delete when it's necessary.

Standout Strategy #2: Do Your Own Thing

Beyond service, you will also set yourself apart from the competition by doing your own thing. Make a point of not doing what everyone else is doing. You've heard that famous old quote, "If you always do what you've always done, you'll always get what you've always gotten." It's been attributed to any number of speakers, and nobody really knows where it originated, but it's a great reminder to change things up and dare to be different.

I hope you will do your best to think outside of the box when it comes to marketing your product. One thing that I've learned over and over and over again while building my own business is

unexpected + unconventional = unforgettable.

If you want people to remember you, you have to give them a reason to do so. Copying everything you see your competition doing won't cut it.

But that sounds so easy, doesn't it? Just do what everyone else isn't doing and voilà—business explosion! Truth be told, it *is* actually that easy—if we don't get in our own way. Actually putting your product out there and talking about it like the expert you are isn't hard. There's just this tendency to second-guess ourselves and judge every single thing we do until fear talks us right out of saying anything at all. We actually can be the problem in our businesses. But if you can get out of our own way, you can do amazing, innovative, unexpected things that really set your business apart.*

One rule when it comes to thinking and working differently is that you'll have to get comfortable being alone. In other words, get comfortable being uncomfortable. Doing something differently and having your tribe around you doing it with you is one thing. Standing up and stepping out on your own with an innovation is an entirely different situation.

You must be confident enough to face the backlash that will come when you put yourself and your different ideas out there. And that backlash will come. I promise you it will.

If I could, I'd physically hold your hand as you push Publish or make your live video explaining your new idea launch. Truly, I would do it if I could, but this is something you're going to have to do on your own. Think back through your stream of consciousness as you brainstormed new ways to market your product or connect with your tribe. How many of them did you dismiss out of fear of being the only one, being different, thinking in a new way?

I'm in the middle of trying to teach my kids this principle right now, and that's really hard to do in elementary school. (Let's face it; it's hard to do at any age.) Last year my youngest daughter was in first grade, and one day she proudly announced that she'd been chosen student of the week. Cue eye roll from mom because as an experienced elementary mom, I just knew that honor was going to involve a home project, and that project

....

* And I mean that in the nicest, most forceful way. It's a requirement, and the more you do it, the easier it becomes. Soon you start to realize the fear feels a whole lot like excitement.

would require pictures, sticky notes, glitter, glue, duct tape, moon rocks, unicorn tail feathers, and number-two pencils shaved to a perfect point.*

I was right. Kennedy pulled out a paper with directions for making her student-of-the-week poster. It was supposed to have pictures from her life along with bedazzles and all the trimmings. In addition, she had to decorate a little cutout girl with God knows what on it.

I stopped reading, and my eyes glazed over at instruction number twenty-seven. I turned to Kennedy and asked her if she'd like to break the rules a little bit and do a project that was a little bit different. I was thinking we could just combine the two and paste her pictures onto a poster cut into the shape of the little girl and call it good. It sounded like a win-win to me—it would save us both the time of working on it all night.

But Kennedy immediately freaked out about the kids in her class knowing her project would be different. Phrases like "Nobody did that, mom" and "That's not what the instructions said" were flying around the kitchen.

I did my best to explain to my daughter how cute it would be and convince her that just because it was going to be different doesn't mean it wouldn't be just as good as (read: better than) the others. She reluctantly complied when I bribed her with chocolate and the threat of "I'm not doing that all night, so it's this or nothing. Get on board."**

We made her poster into the shape of a little girl, and we cut and pasted photos of her life onto it. I'm not going to lie to you—it was freaking adorable. Different, but adorable, and—let's be real—it totally nailed the purpose of the assignment, which was to let her classmates learn a little more about her.

Kennedy went to school the next day still worried about what people would think because her project didn't look like the others. When she got

....

* I loathe kids' school projects at this age because—let's be real—the kids can't do them. It's the parents who end up doing them. And I know, I know, they're only young once—but don't come at me with that at eleven o'clock on a Sunday night as I'm finishing up my kid's project for her.
** Remember what I said about my hard-edge, get-it-done-and-don't-make-excuses attitude? It can be a good thing.

home that afternoon, I asked her how it had gone with her project. Her face lit up and she said, "Mom, everyone said they wanted to do their project like mine from now on."

And now my daughter's not afraid to break the rules when she knows it's not going to hurt her grade or others. She's learned through the school of hard knocks—and a mom who likes to shake things up—that being different is scary, but it can pay off. I have three rule-following children, so I imagine I'll have to teach them this lesson over and over again. I hope you'll do the same for yourself.

Standing out and being different is hard. Being alone is hard. It's also the only real way to improve your product or service. Constant innovation is a necessity in business. Everything about your product or service needs to evolve—how you talk about it, how you present it, how you market it, how you see it. In order to do that properly, you're going to have to step out in front of your competitors from time to time and be alone. It won't be easy, but pretty soon you'll see competitors biting off pieces of your plan and borrowing your innovations. Then you'll know that you've made an impact on your industry—which will be your sign that it's time to innovate again.

Each time I see someone take credit for something I've done or copy it, that's my sign to get back to my desk and think up something new. I hope you'll do the same. Never get too comfortable with what you're doing because change will always be nipping at your heels. Get used to it. Get comfortable with being uncomfortable, comfortable with standing out, comfortable with sometimes being a lone wolf. Love your business and yourself enough to dive right into the deep end.

Standout Strategy #3: Challenge the Status Quo

The most detrimental words in any industry—including yours—are "We've just always done it that way." I hope you hear a record scratch when you read that phrase. I like to think of the status quo as that big paper sign that the cheerleaders hold up for the football players to run through before each game in high school. You know the ones. They're really pretty and they look great. They even serve the purpose of getting the crowd pumped up and setting the tone for the game. But those signs were made to be broken. That's what they're for. And that's how you need to think about what's always been done. You need to ask yourself, *How can I challenge what's always been done? How can I try something new?*

Rethink everything, in other words. Absolutely everything.

Take it apart and put it back together again in a new way.

Challenge the rules. Break them if you have to—even if what you do ruffles a few feathers along the way.*

For inspiration, look at Cards Against Humanity. You know, the company that makes the "party game for horrible people."** Back in 2013, Cards Against Humanity decided they hated the whole Black Friday horribleness.*** (I could not agree more. I am definitely not a fan.) In that spirit they decided to make their hatred of that day into a big joke—to challenge the retail status quo. Instead of putting their product on markdown the day after Thanksgiving like everyone else, they decided to do the opposite and purposely *not* sell their product. In addition, each year they do something outrageous to get customers' attention.

The result? They make their point, they make a bunch of money, and their game gets more attention than ever, making them the undisputed champion of holiday promotions. Here's a sampling of their Black Friday genius:

- In 2013, they sold their game for five dollars *more* than the retail cost of the game to protest Black Friday. Shockingly, sales went up.[4]
- In 2014, they sold actual bull poop packaged in a box. Guys, we're talking literal feces from a real bull. I cannot . . . What's more, thirty-thousand people purchased this, uh, product. They sold out of the boxes in less than two hours.[5]
- In 2015, Cards Against Humanity took their entire store offline and

....

* Just a heads up: the feather ruffling is your sign you're doing something right, you little rebel, you. Now push a little harder. Ruffle some more feathers.
** If you've played this game, you know what I'm talking about. It's the best.
*** I don't think that's a word, but I'm the author here, and that's the kind of power I hold over this book [cue evil laugh].

put up a payment screen where people could give the company five dollars for nothing in return. The result? A total of 11,248 people gave them money for no reason. Nearly 12,000 people gave them more than five dollars. (One person chipped in a hundred bucks.) In the end, they profited $71,145. They then took that money and split it up among their employees to spend on what they would like.[6]

- In 2016, Cards pulled my personal favorite stunt and raised more than a $100,000 to dig a huge hole in the earth, only to immediately fill it right back in. If you were around during that time, you could pay five dollars to the company and watch in real time as a giant tractor took a scoop of dirt out of the earth. And that's all.[7]

- In 2017, this time on Super Bowl Sunday, they decided to rage against the NFL machine and pulled off a fake news stunt wherein they told their customers that they had gone out of business after purchasing a very expensive but unsuccessful (zero dollars in return) ad for the Super Bowl. The commercial was a potato with the word *advertisement* written on it. There was no sound, no movement, nothing else. Just a video of a potato on a white background. People flocked to the Internet to see the ad that cost so much and did so little. In the end, by thinking creatively, they were able to capitalize on the Super Bowl craziness without spending more than the cost of a potato.[8]

If you had asked an industry or marketing expert, she would have surely told you these ideas were horrible, but the stunts accomplished exactly what they were meant to. Cards knew their audience, and they thought outside the box. Their stunts were not without backlash, of course, but they were willing to go alone to do something new, and they not only built better brand recognition but also made good money doing it.

Just think about how many people who read this book will wonder what Cards Against Humanity is cooking up each year during the holidays or big events.

I challenge you to be like them. Don't like the status quo? Change it. You have the power right now to change the game. Remember that we're done with *business as usual*. We're here for the party called *business unusual*.

Standout Strategy #4: Be More Curious

It's important to stay curious when it comes to your product and the people you sell it to. What are they into? Why are they actually buying? Don't assume you know. Instead, have the guts to ask—and be prepared for both the positive and negative answers you will hear.

Requests for improvement may be hard for you to hear because your business is your baby. You've worked tirelessly on it, and it hurts for someone to come along and criticize—as if they don't understand how hard it's been. I totally get that. Nonetheless, I've learned it's important to find out how people honestly feel about your product, about your service, or even about you.

The best question to ask when you're in that curious mind-set is why.

So it's always been done this way. Why?

So it won't work if you break the mold. Why?

Keeping the whys coming and your curiosity open will not only help you put your own self-doubt in check (especially if you write down your answers), but it will also help you deal with people who are trying to get you to conform to the social and cultural norms of your industry.

Being curious about what people want led me to create the LTM Styled Stock Shop (a curated image service) and the Boss Up Box (a quarterly subscription box for CEOs).[9] Both of these are new and small ventures that were born out of my customers telling me, "This is the thing that would help me fix my pain points."

Be curious. And just when you think you've asked enough questions, ask more. Ask as many questions as you need to make sure you are zeroing in on the right improvements to make for your product or service.

Standout Strategy #5: Learn the Lessons from Those Who Came Before You

You don't have to have a formal mentorship in order to glean wisdom from those who came before you or have done what you are dreaming of.

The Internet has made it impossible to *not* have a mentor at this point, even if that person doesn't know your name.

If you watch, study, and listen very closely to the people you admire in business, they'll teach you some shortcuts. They'll give you the keys to their creativity. You'll even get the chance to learn from their mistakes. How can you take what has been started by some of the industry giants in your field and mold it to your target market? What can you learn from how your mentors in your field changed the game to achieve their success?

Never underestimate how much fuel you can inject into your business when you let someone inspire you.

Standout Strategy #6: Nail Things to the Wall; Don't Throw Them

The final way to set yourself apart from the competition has less to do with a home-improvement project and more to do with consistency.

Often you'll hear entrepreneurs say things like "fake it until you make it," and I can understand their sentiment. They mean "say yes and learn along the way," and I can get on board with that. But the problem with that saying is that it can create a lot of inconsistency in your business. If you want to have customers who are constantly using your product or service, the product or service has to consistently be there for them. You have to deliver your product or service every time without question—solid as a rock. This is why you got started and this is what you consistently deliver. If customers start to see you waiver—because you're learning as you go— you won't build loyalty.

Right now I'm in a transition period in my own business. I'm focusing less on the businesses that I have that are now self-sufficient and more on developing my own brand to help female entrepreneurs. This has always been my plan, and it's my heart's work. But as I make that transition, I find it is often confusing for my previous customers who knew me as a group leader, a salesperson, or as a print-shop owner.

I can certainly understand their feelings. But it's up to me to communicate with them (to cut down on the confusion) and also to understand that some people won't be happy for me when I decide to make this change.

Change is difficult in business, especially when it comes to brand-loyal individuals. So I urge you to be cautious when you make change happen. You have to do it, but do it smart and make sure you're nailing things to the wall rather than just throwing things and hoping they stick.

So often I see entrepreneurs shift gears in their businesses and think they've found the next new thing, only to change their minds a couple of months in. Your customers will see that, and they'll remember it. If you're going to make a change, make it stick. Tell your customers how your product or service is going to help them, how you're constantly changing little things to meet their needs, and how much you love what you get to do.

I could write for days on this topic,* and I'd love to sit and talk about all the ways I've seen the unsales tactic transform businesses from business as usual to business unusual in no time at all. It's really not hard. All you really need to remember are the three main pieces of the unsales puzzle:

1. Explore your customers' needs.
2. Understand the things that hold them back.
3. Set your business apart from your competition.

....

* And I totally did, and my editor ripped out half the content because it turns out that what I think is really fun, most people find overwhelming, and my editor hates me. Don't worry. There's another book coming, guys.

SUCCESS PHILOSOPHY #6:
PUT ON YOUR POSITIVE PANTS

It's a Sunday night, and I'm scrolling through Facebook, and I'm missing what I usually feel: a genuine excitement to be alive and able to work. Post after post, meme after meme—the work complaints are downright depressing. And if it's not a dread of Monday or the constant "I need a vacation," it's the faux complaints about being "so busy"—a common but tired gripe meant to make the poster feel important.

We American women are the most blessed and fortunate on the planet. We have the right to work, and, yes, we may get paid less than our male counterparts (for now), but we still get to have jobs and own businesses. We are privileged. We live in a place where women are allowed to follow their dreams. Our potential is limitless.

It's time we act like it.

A couple of years ago, I was in Singapore, taking part in a trade show. It was my second trip there, on the heels of a crushingly disappointing first trip where we were overpromised on the business potential in that area. I don't know if you've ever paid your dues by busting your butt at a trade show, but it's not easy work. And almost five minutes into our day, I had this gut feeling that we were repeating history—that this second trip was going to be just as rough as the first.

The first day felt unbelievably long. My feet hurt. I was tired from the time change. I was *not* excited about my work that day.

As our team was walking out to the car to load all of our stuff for day two, the bellman at the front of our hotel struck up a conversation with us. He was genuinely happy to talk to us and seemed to really love his job. Since it was obvious that we were from out of the country, he asked what we would be doing that day and what we were going to go see. My reply went something like this: "Unfortunately, we have to work today at the convention center." He looked at me like I had seven eyes and said something to me that slapped me in the face, something I'll never forget.

He said, "No, ma'am. With all due respect, *fortunately*, you get to work today."

I wanted to melt into the ground because I realized immediately that (1) he was right and (2) my attitude sucked. And even though the trade show didn't magically go better that day because I'd gotten my ass kicked by a Singaporean bellman that morning, it was, however, a whole lot more enjoyable once my attitude changed.

The Choice to Be Positive

The average person will spend ninety thousand hours at work in their lifetime.[1]

That's a third of our life.

Spent working.

I've heard that how we spend our days is how we spend our life, so we might as well love it. Guess what happens when we love what we do? People want to be a part of it.

If we want to be effective entrepreneurs, therefore—or just decent, reasonably adjusted humans—we need to come up with a genuine excitement for what we do and then show it off. We need to do what we can to be our most positive and happy selves because working in our true selves will cause excitement to ooze out of our pores (and not in a gross way).

This kind of positivity can actually improve your business. It improved mine. My excitement and confidence about my work and my product was a huge factor in getting people pumped to try it too.

Being genuinely excited is rare in our culture. I promise you there are a whole lot more people who hate what they do than love it. Show excitement without hesitation, and I promise it's going to attract people to you and to what you do.

Remember "Oprah's Favorite Things"? Back when the *Oprah Winfrey Show* was still on the air, Oprah would do a Favorite Things episode every year. She would bring a bunch of deserving people into her studio and give away huge prizes to everyone in the audience.

I tuned into that show every year because I wanted to watch positive and happy things happen. I loved watching people get surprised with free cars and other hand-chosen gifts and to see their reactions. It didn't matter that I wasn't the one getting the prizes. I felt good just seeing it happen.

Positivity is contagious, and we all want a little more excitement in our lives. Our lives and our businesses will be better if we consistently seek to surround ourselves with both.

Positivity Policies

My business Facebook group is full of amazing people who do amazing things, but even amazing people must be led and policed when it comes to the Internet. I've learned, in fact, that positivity is far and away the hardest thing to maintain in a large group. This seems to be true with both men and women on the Internet. For some reason we feel compelled to say everything we think behind a computer screen without considering how people on the reading end might be affected.

Most of the policing I do in my groups has to do with my insistence on positivity. I believe in creating and maintaining a culture of positivity, but that's not easy, especially online. I've found I must be willing to be the bad guy in order to maintain it, and that I actually have to train my people how to do it. At one point I even did a series of posts—"Twenty-one Days of Positivity"—based on a TED Talk by the amazingly brilliant and kind

Shawn Achor, who will blow your mind and make you a believer in the effects of positive psychology.[2]

One of my rules for my business is that I will never complain in a public forum, online or otherwise. I recommend this same policy for you. Serious words are sometimes necessary, but they shouldn't happen where the public (especially customers) see it. Take your conversation offline so you can deal specifically with your customer and solve their difficulties if possible.

Running a business with an online presence means we need to present ourselves as both positive and professional everywhere we interact. This isn't always obvious to people, especially those who are new to business and not used to being under a microscope. We need to put some thought and discipline into making sure we are consistently representing what our brand is supposed to be. (In my groups that means being caring, fun, positive, helpful, and encouraging.)

All this means we need to think twice about anything we write or say, especially in a business context. Before hitting Post or Publish, consider:

1. Will this build others up?
2. Will it be helpful to my customers, my colleagues, or both?
3. Will it inspire trust?
4. Will it contribute to my success and the success of my tribe?

If not, maybe you're better off not posting it.

As a young girl, I remember being taught an acronym in school to help me T.H.I.N.K. before I speak. As an adult, I find holding my tongue as difficult as I did as a kid, so I find the little mnemonic helpful. It reminds me to ask, "Is what I'm about to say . . ."

T = True?
H = Helpful?
I = Inspiring?
N = Necessary?
K = Kind?

I know none of this is new to you. But it's so easy to forget when our feelings are hurt or our ego rears its ugly head. When someone spreads a rumor or writes something hurtful either about me or to me, my instinct is to stick up for myself, to defend what I do and how I do it. I know I'm prone to snap back when someone says something hurtful or untrue to me or others. But the truth is my angry or frustrated responses rarely improve the situation. More often it makes things worse.

One of the policies I insist on in all my groups is that complaints go up, not down. A scene from a small, obscure little indie film called *Saving Private Ryan* (maybe you've heard of it) explains this principle beautifully:

Private Reiben: Hey, so, Captain, what about you? I mean, you don't gripe at all?

Captain Miller: I don't gripe to *you,* Reiben. I'm a captain. There's a chain of command. Gripes go up, not down. Always up. You gripe to me, I gripe to my superior officer, so on, so on, and so on. I don't gripe to you. I don't gripe in front of you. You should know that as a Ranger.

Private Reiben: I'm sorry, sir, but uh . . . let's say you weren't a captain, or maybe I was a major. What would you say then?

Captain Miller: Well, in that case . . . I'd say, "This is an excellent mission, sir, with an extremely valuable objective, sir, worthy of my best efforts, sir. Moreover . . . I feel heartfelt sorrow for the mother of Private James Ryan and am willing to lay down my life and the lives of my men—especially you, Reiben—to ease her suffering."

Mellish: [chuckles] He's good.

Private Caparzo: I love him.[3]

You see how it works? Complaints need to be directed up to the person who can actually do something about them, not down where they can bring everyone down.

I am not saying you have to hold everything inside to be falsely cheerful when you're really blue and depressed. It really doesn't have to be all cupcakes and rainbows—you can still be yourself and talk honestly about things that concern you. But your social media feed and conversations with others should not be filled with gripes about what you're annoyed with, what you hate, what (or who) you can't stand to look at, or how hard everything is.

After all, people need a reason to want to be around you—you *need* them around you, *especially* when you're feeling down. Constant negativity and complaints don't do anything but turn people off to your business, your brand, and maybe even yourself.

Let me say for the record: any complaints that make it into my online groups are dealt with privately and deleted.

My group. My rules.

And if this causes issues with people who like to get online and spew a bunch of negativity, well, I'm okay with that. I'm perfectly willing to let my competition deal with those guys.

Positive and Professional

I want you to understand that while I value positivity, I'm not necessarily a positive person, at least not all the time. I can be stubborn (surprise). I tend to think I can do things faster and more efficiently by myself. I don't particularly like being criticized. And when I'm frustrated or mad about something, the last thing I want to be is positive and rational. I wanna be all, "B, you don't know my life!" and kick my computer screen. I can say to you, from personal experience, that it's really hard to maintain a positive attitude and excitement when a lot of people come at you just to complain.

Trust me, as a business owner, I get lots of complaints. So will you. People won't read directions. They'll skip steps. They'll forget to do important stuff. And I really want to help them, but I can only take so much. That kind of ongoing negativity takes a toll on me, as I know it does for you too.

That's why I live by the rule that any complaint that arises must be followed by two solutions. Believe me, this is difficult when I don't want to be rational or when I'm worn out by complaints. But I know that bringing at least two ideas or solutions to the table will go further toward solving the problem, and it also invites the other person to jump in and help me solve the problem too.

Finally, something to keep in mind as you interact with other business owners or customers online is that you need to make choices for your business based on the information you have, and others need to do the same. Make sure you're thinking of and treating your business like a business. That means staying professional with your people, even if they're your friends. That means making decisions based on professional and not personal concerns.

I really want you to keep in mind that you are running a business now (yay!) and that ultimately you are responsible for its success. That may mean making hard decisions that might be great for you but won't be what the people around you want. Not fun, I know, but you have to do what is right for your own business—including setting the tone for your operation and enforcing it.

Think about the kind of environment you want for your business and set out to be the example of that through your own groups, teachings, and interactions. Are you allowing your work environment to be a dumping ground for complaints and negativity? That will just breed more of the same. Don't let it happen.

Yes, there will be people who won't be able to get on board with your attempts to keep things positive. It's up to you to have the guts not to let them infect the overall happiness of your group. And, yes, both positivity and negativity can be contagious. As Shawn Achor explains, that fact is rooted in biology:

> If a brain is scanned while someone is smiling, small parts of the brain called mirror neurons light up. If you show someone a photo of someone who is smiling, those mirror neurons fire, tell your brain that you are the one smiling, and your mouth responds with a smile. It's like yawning. . . .

Not only do smiles and yawns spread, so does negativity. If we're in the midst of negativity, others pick it up like second-hand smoke. It's the same way our brains process the world. . . .

The human brain is actually designed to work better when it is positive, rather than negative, neutral or stressed—as shown in improvements in scores on 10 different types of intelligence tests, i.e. spatial, verbal reasoning, quantitative. Studies also show that priming subjects to be positive increases performance on the job. For example, happy doctors create 19% faster and more accurate diagnoses, and show three times more intellectual flexibility of misdiagnoses.[4]

We must help our customers, groups, employees, and coworkers change their way of thinking and teach them how to see stresses, obstacles, and unforeseen circumstances in business as challenges instead of threats. There will always be issues, but we must strive to create an environment that produces solutions instead of wallowing in disappointment.

PRO TIP

Here are some suggestions to help get yourself into a positive mind-set when you're feeling less than positive:

1. **Make a list of a few things you're grateful for right now.** I find that when I focus on the things I'm thankful for in my life, I can't focus on what's not going right.
2. **Take the time to hand-write a love note** to a member of your family and put it somewhere that person will find it that day.
3. **Bust out Headspace or another meditation app** and do ten minutes of meditation and prayer. Or do it the old-fashioned way and simply pray.
4. **Journal about how you're feeling.** I find that when I write down the things I'm fearful of, they become a lot less scary.

5. **Go outdoors.** Walk around the block or take a bike ride for a few minutes to get some fresh air and a new perspective.
6. **Write down a positive affirmation to combat your negative self-talk.** Speak your affirmation out loud in the mirror.
7. **Change your environment.** Maybe today is the day to work on the back porch instead of in the office to give yourself a fresh perspective.
8. **Organize a single space** in your home or office to help you gain a feeling of accomplishment and simplicity.
9. **Call your most positive friend,** someone who can speak some truth into your situation.
10. **Go crazy.** Play hooky and go to lunch or to a movie. Get in bed and read a book during the middle of the day, just to shake things up.

Positivity can be learned—so teach your tribe how to be positive. Model your own positivity as well. Be diligent about keeping your work environment as happy and helpful as possible. Help your customers and online business groups remain solution focused by walking through problems with them, and be consistent about making them come to you with possible solutions. The truth is you can't afford not to have a positive work environment; your success and your work happiness depend on it.

Honest Can Be Positive

So I've told you to be positive, but I've also told you to be yourself. If I were you, my next question would be, *How do I get honest about hard stuff while staying positive?*

I've seen many entrepreneurs jump on the "vulnerability train" and try to make up things to be vulnerable about. And it always feels off. Right now, I see so many business owners using fake vulnerability ("vulnerable post alert" or "I'm so scared to admit this, you guys") to gain attention rather than using what's actually real and imperfect for connection.

There's a thin line between being authentic about the hard parts of your life and dumping all your issues onto your followers, but it's worth the effort to walk that line successfully. I believe the key to being honest and authentic about the not-so-positive stuff is your intent. Is your intent to help people by letting them in on your difficult situation, or is it to get attention or unload your misery on others? The audience will feel that intent, I guarantee.

To drive this point home, I'm about to give you guys a little peek into my bedroom. If adult, married, consensual sex makes you freak out, now is the time to turn the page because sex is a big thing between Michael and me. If we are ever in a fight or we find ourselves perpetually annoyed with the presence of the other, you can guarantee it's been a couple of days since we've made out. And if that couple of days should turn into a few more, I have this awful habit of starting to think terrible thoughts about myself. *Maybe he's over me. Crap, are we doing okay? Maybe I'm too fat. Maybe I'm not worth the effort.*[*]

Just by my writing that down, I know how crazy and dramatic it sounds. But sex helps Michael and me function as one rather than two. That's the point.

The thing is I have such a fear of vulnerability that I don't ordinarily tell Michael where my thoughts have been. Instead, I just keep feeling unwanted and alone, and that leads to more disconnection between us.

Recently, though, I decided to be an adult and show a little weakness and tell him where I was in order to fuel connection rather than perpetuate disconnection. And, of course, we talked it through and got ourselves back on track because he doesn't feel about me the way I often feel about myself . . . duh.

True vulnerability can help you actually connect to your people (and followers) if you're brave enough to face and discuss the shadows and imperfections of your life. And friends, that's a positive, not a negative.

....

* I know, I know. TMI. Yet I'm pretty sure I'm not alone in this kind of thinking.

You can avoid the Internet's terrible example of fake vulnerability by being authentically vulnerable. Pull back the curtains on the thoughts, feelings, and actions you usually deal with alone. Connect with your people.

Last week I actually cried on social media for the first time ever. I was freaked out about putting my face on the cover of this book and about the reaction I might get when targeting moms, who—let's face it—can be a touch on the judgy side. *I'm not a size two,* I reminded myself (as if I could forget). *What will people say? Everybody likes to look at attractive, thin, happy women on the covers of books, but what about happy women who aren't thin? Will my physical appearance ruin my chance to get this book into the hands of my audience? Is this the right choice?* So many questions bred from fear and insecurity raced through my mind as I recorded that post, and soon I was crying.

The tears were real, and it was so hard to hit the post button. But I did. I told my story of fear and let my audience in on my struggle—not to solicit pity or encouragement, but to show that we're all more alike than we are different.

The story didn't just stop there though. It had to keep going in order for me to use it for good. So the next day, after I had a conversation with God and some people I trust, I picked myself up and did another post. By that time I'd been able to change my attitude and mind-set about those things I was most afraid of, and I was able to show that to my audience as well.

Not that I'm not still afraid. I am—trust me, I am. But the example for my tribe is that we all face real fear and we have to walk into it, not away from it. That fear was holding up a mirror to my own self-doubt and self-esteem—things I have to work on, places where I struggle. But in facing and sharing that struggle, I made an authentic (and positive) connection with my people.

People are going to say what they say no matter what size my jeans are. I can't let that hold me back from using my voice. I am not a number on the scale. I am not disqualified from talking about any subject just because I may do it differently than others choose to do it. I am enough, right now—and I needed to remember that.

And do you know what? The responses I received most frequently after those posts were "Me too." and "You're not alone." My intent in posting my most vulnerable and difficult moments on social media was to connect to others through my struggle, to encourage them and help them realize the truth—that we are all more alike than different. Apparently it worked. And the interesting thing is that it ended up helping me too.

Nothing has brought my insecurities to the surface like owning my own business. Being a momtrepreneur just pushes me in so many ways. The same will likely be true for you. But through authentically sharing our stories and our struggle, we can end up turning a possible negative into a positive.

Two Sides of Selling

Make no mistake. Everything you put into the world from your brand is something to be sold. The act of putting it out there is "selling." And sales sometimes gets a bad rap; it's associated with sleaziness, pushiness, and manipulation. But we sell things all the time without a hint of sleaze.

When you try to convince your family to get Chick-fil-A for dinner so you can drink a gallon of Chick-fil-A sauce, you're selling to them.*

When you talk to your friends about the new Dyson hairdryer you bought, you're a salesperson for that product.

You're not doing it because you can't wait to take advantage of your friends or family. You're doing it because you like the product and you want your people to like it too.

Selling is only gross if you don't believe in the product, service, or idea you're selling. You don't need to feel any guilt or shame around sales. You should, however, give some thought to *how* you're selling and how your sales techniques can affect people.

....

* But again, you don't need to sell something that everybody already wants. You just simply present the value to them: "If you do not go with me to Chick-fil-A, your life will be in danger!" See? Works every time.

There are basically two general approaches to selling. There's the positive side and the negative side.

When you, as a salesperson, use the positive side, you show people how your product can make their lives easier, healthier, more fulfilled, and less stressed—how the product meets their needs and makes their lives better. When you go negative, on the other hand, you show what could go wrong if the customer *doesn't* buy the product.

Now, there is a way to do negative sales right. But there is a very thin line between using the negative the right way and going overboard, shaming and scaring the customer. We've all seen this kind of negative marketing in our social media feeds and on the news. It's called fear mongering. And it's a great way to make people mad.

Have you ever felt uneasy, even angry, about a story of tragedy used by a brand to sell their product? At the same time, have you ever felt more connected to a brand because a tragic but authentic story moved you? I have felt both. The difference between these polar-opposite reactions, I believe, is the intent behind the story being told.

There's a television commercial now targeting mothers that starts with a shot of a woman looking sullen and filled with shame. She holds up cards with her story of tragedy on them and lets them fall to the floor as sad music plays. She even begins to weep about how she basically let her daughter down and damaged her body by not getting the correct vaccine for her. She was the mom, and she could have prevented the tragedy but didn't. Then she gets up from the table to reveal her teenage daughter wearing a sports uniform, looking as sad as humanly possible, and revealing a prosthetic leg. Mother and daughter walk out of the house as if they're disappointed that they have to go on living like this. If only the mother had been better at protecting her child! (Insert eye roll here).

Obviously the intent of this commercial is to stir up worry in the hearts of the mothers who are watching so they'll make the decision to vaccinate their daughters. It's supposed to make them feel they'll be terrible mothers if they don't and to feel super ashamed. But that's not how that commercial makes me feel. What it actually does is make me super mad—because the marketers are taking advantage of how much they *know*

I love my kids. They're saying that if I don't buy their product, then I'll be purposely hurting my kids. I would never, ever buy that product because of the manipulative negative marketing that uses a tragic story to make us feel scared as consumers so they can turn more profit.

On the other hand, Allstate insurance uses tragedy to sell their product without eliciting that manipulated feeling inside me. Have your seen the ones that feature Dean Winters as "Mayhem," exposing all of the places in your lives where we need a good insurance company. My favorite one is where Mayhem becomes "the world's worst cleaning lady," breaking all the valuables in the house and eventually falling down the stairs on a loose rug. The ad, of course, is selling home insurance to help cover the medical bills for accidents that happen to other people inside your home. Like the vaccine ad, it warns of possible tragedy, but it's done in a way where I don't feel manipulated or shamed to buy the product.

The Allstate ads manage to walk that successful line and use negative marketing effectively, but that's really hard to do. Don't play on your customers' fears. They aren't stupid, and they see right through attempts to play on their fears by going negative. Once that happens, the trust you're trying to build will be broken. And trust, remember, is ultimately what sells your product.

I like to think of negativity in sales as being like salt in a recipe. A little bit goes a long way, and too much could ruin a recipe. Most of the time, I believe, you'll be better with a positive approach.

Positive Crisis Management

I recently hired a local, female-run company to help me design some built-in cabinets for one of the rooms in my house. I had worked with the designer—we'll call her Mary—when we moved into our house in Denver. I'd really liked working with her. She was smart, worked fast, communicated well, and did a great job helping me get the things I needed for the house. But this time, as soon as I paid the down payment for her services and the product, Mary started to drop the ball. Halfway through the project she went radio silent. Broken product showed up at my house, and the final price went way over her original bid. Overall, I was super unhappy with how this business transaction went down.

When we confronted Mary about her poor service, she became super upset and combative. She started to cry, started calling us names to protect herself, placed blame everywhere but on her own shoulders, and basically made the situation way worse than it had been even a few minutes before our talk. Clearly she had no idea how to handle crises with her customers. She didn't know how to own the problems she had created or how to make them better. Eventually Mary lost the job because it turned out there were other customers she had hung out to dry on their projects as well.

That company now has a huge mess on its hands and is going to have to try to make it right. This is a crisis for the owner of this company. Even if she was diligent about taking care of her customers, her employee wasn't.

No matter how positively you approach your business and your customers, at some point a crisis will arise. It could be a customer who leaves a bad review. It could be a series of accidents or a downturn in the market. It could even be that a disruptor comes along and changes the game before you've reached your goals. When that happens, your challenge is dealing with the crisis in the right way so it doesn't damage the work you've done or your reputation among your customers and followers.

Welcome to the world of entrepreneurship. At some point, it's going to feel like you're taking it from all sides. That's just part of owning your own business.

Effective crisis management, the process by which an organization or an entrepreneur deals with any major event that threatens to harm it, is one of the most underrated skills in business. We need to be professionals in crisis management just as we are in sales.

Let's say someone suddenly accuses you and your product of harming them in some way. They're raising a big stink. If you're not prepared for this kind of crisis, just that e-mail or phone call could make you start to panic. Worse, it could make you get defensive with the customer, and that will only serve to aggravate them more. Now it's you against them, and trust me, you don't want to go there until you have to.

Personally, I almost always get super mad first when something like that happens because I know the customer hasn't seen how hard I've worked to create a product that works for everyone who purchases it. I've had to learn to talk myself down from there because my response to a crisis can determine whether the outcome is positive or negative for my company. That's something you need to learn as well.

When an e-mail comes in that says, "I hate your product, I hate you, and I'm going to the Internet to let everyone know you're the spawn of Satan," the first thing you need to do is not panic. Do not write back immediately. Take some time to chill out and possibly put yourself in the disgruntled customer's shoes. Show some empathy for the fact that they purchased your product or service and it didn't turn out like they thought. You've probably been on that side of the fence before—hopefully without the name calling and terrible use of words.

Once you've calmed down, there are steps you can take to deal with your crisis in the most productive and positive way possible. What you need to do is this:

1. **Be calm and be you.** Talk to the customer like they're a normal person who is trying their best to make informed decisions about a product they likely don't know a lot about. Even though they're upset, they are putting a lot of trust in you to help them do this. Do your best to be worthy of that trust.

2. **Empathize.** "**If I had the experience you did, I'd probably be upset too, so I'd like to apologize right up front.** That is not the kind of experience I want my customers to have with my company." Right here you've told them you understand, you don't judge them for coming to you, and (subtly) that you have more experience.

3. **Concisely—and I do mean concisely—give them facts** about what's behind the issue they're having and, if possible, what you're going to do to make sure they're happy.

4. **If you cannot do anything to fix the issue, make sure you offer to make it right financially for them.** That way, hopefully, you

can retain them as a future customer. Offer them information about what you are going to do to make sure that their issue doesn't happen to anyone else.

5. **Whatever you do, don't start popping off with the blame game.** "Well, let me tell you about this drama and that drama and what they did and how this is all their fault." Just state the facts. Be reasonable, calm, and kind. It's okay to give them a quick version of your story so they know your character, but don't overload them with huge dissertations about all that you do and how this has never, ever happened before. Just let them know you wouldn't put out an inferior product or service if you knew about it, and make it clear how seriously you take your job.

Let's not use any crisis or disaster as fodder to get worked up about something. Don't bring it to your colleagues, team, or outsiders if there's no need. Why would you get everyone worked up? Just chill. Think rationally. Is this really that big that you have to make people worry about it, or is it going to fade?

I sometimes find entrepreneurs use crisis to avoid doing work for the day. They just get so caught up that they can't concentrate on getting back to work because there might be another human out there who hasn't heard about the situation. (Just calling that spade a spade, friends.) Crisis is not the place to spend all of your time. Get in, fix it, and get out.

Above all—and I'll say it again—do your very best to stay positive. Remind yourself, as the Singaporean bellman reminded me, that you are indeed fortunate to get to do this work you do.

So go. Be excited. Stop apologizing for being excited and confident about what you do. Instead, let your positivity lift up everyone around you and get them excited too.

10

SUCCESS PHILOSOPHY #7: KEEP LEARNING

I am quite certain this is the philosophy that was hardest for me to grasp, learn, and lean into. And there's a good reason for that: my personality.

Have you taken the Enneagram test yet? If not, it's time. It's going to blow your mind.* I'm an 8 with a wing of 7. That basically means that I'm the bossiest people person on the planet. It also means that I tend to see changing my mind or putting myself in the vulnerable position of being wrong as weakness—and I hate weakness. For us 8 types, weakness is our kryptonite.

The truth is that it took many years of making terrible choices for my life and my businesses to convince me that I should probably humble myself and take the time to learn a thing or two. In order for me to get better at being an entrepreneur, I have to admit that I don't know it all, that not having all the answers isn't weakness, and that changing my mind doesn't make me a bad business owner.

I hope you don't take as long as I did to realize all this. The truth is

....

* My favorite test costs twelve dollars at www.enneagraminstitute.com, and it's been worth every penny invested in learning about how people see me and how people often misunderstand me.

your business is going to be a constant schooling for you if you innovate as you should along the way. It is imperative that you don't get stuck— that you keep learning. It's the only way for your business to evolve. It should not look the same now as it will ten years down the road. You will have to adapt and change as our environment, culture, and customers change.

This also means that you'll make mistakes, and many of them will happen publicly. You'll fall right on your face for your customers to see— for the Internet to see. And that's okay—it really is. Let go of that pride, sister, because entrepreneurship is not likely to be great for your ego.

Nothing has ever made me feel less sure of myself than going first with a new idea as a business owner. It's like running on Jell-O—a whole lot of running around and not a lot of movement on a day-to-day basis. Which always makes me worry: "Is this even working? Is this the right change?" I was probably right to worry because I messed up a lot. So will you.

The truth is, if you're doing business right, mistakes are inevitable. But if you're doing it right, you're also learning from those mistakes. Get up, dust yourself off, maybe drink a bottle of wine, and move on.

Be Coachable

A great way to keep learning throughout life is to be coachable. Humble. Teachable. And that's actually a remarkable accomplishment in a world where there's pressure to have it all figured out. It takes admitting you're wrong at times. It takes setting your ego aside. It takes realizing you don't have an answer. It takes changing your mind sometimes.

Oh my gosh, you guys. I want so badly to have all the answers. I want to know the right thing to do and the right time to do it. I don't like having to ask for help. And I really, really hate being told what to do. Here's just one example of just how much I hate it.

A few years back (just a few), on my twenty-first birthday, a group of my friends drove from Phoenix to San Diego for the weekend to celebrate.

One of those friends was my boyfriend of five years.* We got to San Diego, and a couple of my girlfriends started talking about going to get tattoos. And I was in because I've always been that girl. Always up for something a little bit scary and a little bit fun (read: risk taker).

Immediately my boyfriend interjected and told me not to get a tattoo because he didn't want me to.** You can guess how well that went down. I marched my twenty-one-year-old butt down to the closest tattoo place, pointed to the first arbitrary design on the wall, and told the dude behind the counter to put it on my ankle. I then walked back to the house where we were all staying with a grin on my face. Because nobody was going to tell me what to do.

So I now have a shooting star that looks a little like a mix between a snake and a whip permanently attached to my body. Face. Palm.

I call it my spite tattoo.

Yes, I got a tattoo out of spite because I am so opposed to being told what to do.

What. A. Tool. I. Am.

You'll be happy to know I've come a long way since then. I still don't think it's cool for a boyfriend to have any say in what his girlfriend chooses for her body. (There are reasons that relationship didn't last.) But I'm a lot better now about choosing which instruction to take and how to react when someone gives it to me.

In the same way, I'm working my way out of being a stubborn, hard-headed business owner. I'm learning to lay down my "I've got this" attitude and become more coachable. I'm learning that I need people who know more than I do and have been in my shoes to give me advice at times. And while I still have a visceral response when someone tells me what to do or how I have to do it, I've learned that I do my business a disservice when I resist being coachable. I need mentors to come alongside me and tell me, "Lindsay, you're being an idiot. Don't do that," or "Lindsay, you're not seeing the whole picture here."

....

* Not Michael, for the record, #MarriedUp.
** Beware of boyfriends who tell you what to do.

Learn to Detach

These days I'm so grateful when someone is willing to come alongside me and my business and lay out some truth for me. I've learned how to process that information in the right way. I've also done a better job in the last few years separating my personal worth from my business success. That's called detachment, and it is really important.

Let's talk about detachment for a second because it's a huge part of becoming coachable, of laying aside ego and hurt feelings in the name of learning.

Detachment basically means disconnecting your accomplishments and failures (including business wins and losses) from who you are and how valuable you are. This is something I see so few women do. Detachment also means severing the tie between who you are and the label the Internet puts on you—realizing that other people's opinions are theirs and have no bearing on what is actually true about you.

Learning detachment can help you get on board with being coached or getting constructive criticism because that criticism has nothing to do with your intrinsic worth. Other people's opinions don't change your right to own your business and reach success. In fact, you need those opinions to give you perspectives you may not have considered. We need other people with different world views and different experiences to speak into our businesses and our lives.

There are so many places in our life where we need to learn detachment—from goals, certainty, and other people's opinions, to physical and mental discomfort, drama, greatness, and perfection (just to name a few). That doesn't mean you don't care about these things—simply that you realize they don't define you. You are worthy no matter what other people say and how many goals you hit. As I've said before and I'll continue to say, you are enough.

Detachment is not the same as shirking responsibility for our wins and our losses—after all, taking responsibility for these is also a big part of how we learn and grow. But detachment does mean we quit tying those wins and losses to our value as human beings, that we quit seeing ourselves as less valuable when things don't go as planned or when we fail.

You are not the sum of your wins and losses in this life. You are uniquely and wonderfully made, no matter if you win or lose.

Be Willing to Change Your Mind and Make Mistakes

How many of us made grand statements about parenting before we actually had kids? Oh, I did, my friends. I did.

I love asking moms about this: "Tell me one thing you thought you'd never do as a mom that you have done." That question puts us all on an even playing field because we've all been there, and we all can relate.

Here's my own list of things I said I'd never do as a mom, back when I knew nothing of what it meant to raise a child with a mind of her own:

1. **My kid will never wear themed character clothing.** One way for my kids to get anything they want is to give the cute face to their dad or to ask me for that Snow White shirt approximately 264 times in one hour.

2. **I won't let my kids experience more than a half hour of screen time in a day.** Oh, how naive I was. Sometimes I need a break so that my head doesn't spin around in a full circle a la *The Exorcist*.

3. **I won't let my kids leave the house with crazy hair and insane clothing choices.** I thought it would be so easy to get children ready to leave the house. But now I know that if I insisted on my kids letting me do their hair and wear the clothes I like best, we'd be at least seven hours late for everything we do.

4. **I'll lose the baby weight once the baby (or in my case babies) come.** "Hahahahahahahahaha—okay, lady!" my saddlebags said.

You guys have heard the slogan from the diaper company Luvs, right? Their entire brand statement—"Live and learn and then get Luvs"—is wrapped around the idea that we all think we have it figured out until we actually experience reality. That statement says, "Sure, friend, go grab those expensive diapers for your first child. We'll see you when you're a little more educated about what your child actually needs and how much you're willing to spend on diapers."

That idea applies to a lot more than diapers. There are so many areas of life—business included—where we all think we have it figured out, then realize all the things we didn't know. If we're smart, we respond to that shock by living and learning. We change our minds, pick up new skills, and move forward.

I love what Malcom Gladwell had to say about this: "That's your responsibility as a person, as a human being—to constantly be updating your positions on as many things as possible. And if you don't contradict yourself on a regular basis, then you're not *thinking*."[1]

I used to think that making mistakes and changing my mind made me weak or unwise. I believed people would take me more seriously if I stood firm to my original thought or feeling. That's not the truth though. I've learned that, in life and in business, we just don't know what we don't know. Most of us are walking through unique, new situations where we don't know the outcome of every decision we make. We have to give ourselves room to about-face and change our minds if what we thought would work just does not.

The fastest way to run your business into the ground is to assume you always have the answers inside you and that each decision you make is the right one. Each of us only has so much experience and skill. We need to seek out others who can hold up a mirror to the things we can't see so we can make the most educated decisions for our business.

Your ability to change your mind and make mistakes means you've learned to set aside your ego. That is the kind of person who attracts others. At times I've been so ego fueled in my business life that I was unwilling to let go of opinions and ideas that no longer served me and that I no longer believed. But as I've fed my mind with great books and amazing people, I've realized I am just not as good by myself as I am with others who help me realize what I don't know. In the process I've learned to ease up on my ego, listen, and learn—at least more than I used to. And this has made me freer, more flexible, and more confident.

I recommend the same for you. Let's own our mistakes, change our minds, and let others see us do it. That way we're a part of changing the narrative around perfection in business.

Mentorship: Find One

To reach the top in our businesses, we will need to stand on the shoulders of giants. There's so much to learn from the people who have come before us because they've experienced more than we have. Remember, there is no way for one person to have all the answers, and often the best course of action is to get some good advice.

Mentors help us reach our full potential. Nobody has ever reached success without the help of another person. Or, in my case, hundreds of people. Mentors have been so important in my journey as a mother and as being guides in my business.

A mentor is simply someone who can speak truth into your life and help guide you on the path to living well. And there are many different varieties of mentorship. You may be fortunate enough to still consider your parents mentors in your life as an adult. You may have different spiritual mentors, marriage and motherhood mentors, academic mentors. And then of course there are business mentors, which are our focus here. The two types of business mentorship I'm going to focus on are the formal (one-on-one) and informal (large group).

Mentorship Type #1: One-on-One Mentorships

A one-on-one mentorship is created when you build a deliberate working relationship with someone who has experience to share or wisdom you may need. This may be set up formally or informally. Meetings may be face-to-face or via technology. But the two people in the mentoring relationship get to know each other personally.

These relationships are almost never built by sending an e-mail to someone you don't know, someone who has no investment in you as a business professional, asking them "Will you be my mentor?" To be honest, I've never said yes to such a request, and I don't expect I'd get many people to agree to mentor me that way, either. I think the relationship has to be established first for someone to dedicate that kind of time to me and my success. (The kinds of formal mentorship programs that sometimes exist in the corporate world seem to be rare or nonexistent in the world of entrepreneurship.)

So how do you find a one-on-one mentor? You do have the option to seek out a business coach and pay for their services. Having someone to consult for advice as you grow is a great advantage. Make sure you know what you're getting into, though, as the financial and time requirements will vary by program. Business coaches can be either a great experience or a complete let-down, in my experience. Do your research and make wise choices about where to spend your hard-earned money if you're going to pay for a business coach.

As for finding a mentor through networking, this is one area where I would advise you not to follow my example. I'm just going to come right out and tell you that finding this kind of mentor has been one of the biggest struggles in my business. I didn't even think to look for one until I had already built a large business—honestly, I thought I just didn't have time. I was head-down into growing my business, working but not networking. In retrospect, that was probably a mistake, but that's what happened.

Lack of time wasn't the only thing that held me back from pursuing a one-on-one mentorship though. Insecurity played a part as well. I would ask myself why someone who had made their millions and paid their dues would even bother with someone like me. So I didn't (and still don't) tend to reach out to people I look up to in the business world. I hang back when someone I admire is in the room. That's *my* confidence problem. I hope you don't make it yours.

Remember, I'm not talking about reaching out and asking for a mentorship. I'm talking about making deliberate connections with people you look up to and want to know better. That is how most mentorships start, and I find it really difficult to do that. I'm more likely just to stay silent and small because I assume I'm not worthy of other people's time.

Real talk: I also think finding a one-on-one mentor as a woman can be difficult. I often find men pulling back from having a mentorship role with me, and I have to believe it's because it might be a little awkward for a married man and a married woman to have that kind of close working relationship. And the pool of experienced female business mentors is much smaller than that of their male counterparts. Add that to the list of things I'd like to change.

Still, as tough as it may be to find this kind of mentorship, I'd encourage you to seek it out. Build relationships with people you think are further down the road than you are. Follow them. Reach out to them. Let them know what they do that resonates with you. Ask them questions without taking up too much of their time at the beginning. And give them what you do have—you. You have a unique perspective. You are the only you. And I believe someone will come along who will take a special interest in your success if you put yourself out there and go first.

Mentorship Type #2: Large-Group Mentorships

I'm no stranger to this kind of mentorship. It's the kind where you go out and find that handful of people who freely give the thing you need—advice. The Internet, for instance, is an amazing source of guidance where you can have access to some of business's greatest minds with the click of a few buttons. Books, periodicals, and conferences can be great mentoring resources too. You don't even have to know your mentors!

I've been mentored by some amazing minds in this way: Seth Godin, Donald Miller, Jen Hatmaker, Jon Acuff, Ryan Holiday, Ray Dalio, Shawn Achor, Stephen Covey, Daniel Pink, Amy Cuddy, Brené Brown, and so many more. (I've met only one of those people in person.) These men and women mentor me as they open their business playbooks for others at the same time.

And I pay attention! I read their books, their social media posts, and the e-mails they send their subscribers. I watch or listen to their live videos, podcasts, and interviews and seek out opportunities to hear them speak. I write down the wisdom they share with the world and apply what works for me. I especially note the things they say that fly in the face of what I believe, and I try to get curious about the things that make me defensive. I let them teach me from afar even though most of them have no idea who I am.

I read a book by Jon Acuff in 2015 that inspired my husband and me to take a big risk and move our family from Seattle, Washington, to Salt Lake City. Without even knowing us at the time, Jon guided us through that decision and gave us the confidence to make that choice, which was one of the single greatest risks we have ever taken. We only ended up living in Utah for a year and a half, but the relationships I built during that time in my career helped me take my business to the next level. And it all happened because Jon took the time to put his ideas about entrepreneurship into the world.

I will always be grateful for his guidance, and I pray that my efforts to share what I've learned might help someone the same way. Even at a distance, mentorship can change the course of a life and a business.

Mentorship: Be One

As important as it is to find a mentor to guide you on your road to success, being a mentor who guides others is important as well. To make an impact on the generation of business owners that comes after us, we all have to be willing to open up our playbooks and teach them what we've learned. Just make sure the timing is right.

There was a time in my professional life when I did not have the margin to focus outside of my own business. I was working crazy hours to reach some really big goals. I was laser focused on building my team and helping the customers in my organization. Plus, I had three little kids at home and a husband who worked long hours as well.

Suffice to say that was not the right time for me to take on a mentorship role. There weren't enough extra hours or even minutes in my day-to-day routine to make that happen, so I decided to opt out of mentoring others. And this decision caused some backlash for me during that time. But I still believe it was the right choice—both for me and the person I would have been mentoring.

Trust me: there will be times of growth for you, and there will be times to help others grow. Don't you dare feel any kind of guilt if it's not your time to take on a mentee. That's a serious commitment. The time has to be right, and you have to have a real interest in growing another person's business. Without that, a mentorship just will not work.

Your time to pass on what you have learned will come. It came for me, and I found that when I was ready, I couldn't *not* do it. Last year I took on paid mentorships. I mentored my followers through the content I created, and I took a special interest in a few people I wanted to help grow because we had built that kind of relationship with one another.

I know it's finally my time to take on the mentor role because I now have more margin in my day and also because my heart has shifted from growing my business to having a deep desire to influence others to do the same.

When your own time comes for being a mentor, keep in mind that there are many ways to do it. Don't pigeonhole yourself into taking on a particular kind of mentorship if it's not something you love. I have a good friend who's a brilliant inventor and entrepreneur. He was taking on one-on-one coaching clients, but when I asked if he liked it, he said, "No, not really, I probably won't keep doing this." He'd rather spend his time mentoring the employees who work for him directly than coaching clients in different fields.

Choices like that are your prerogative too. Your business. Your life. Your choice. Go do what is right for you. But someday, if you feel that call to help another person on her road to success, don't ignore it. You won't just help her grow, but you, yourself, will grow as well.

Say More Yes

Do you remember the first day of your first job? I remember mine.

I was freshly sixteen years old when I got a job at a bead store in Tempe,

Arizona, called Another Bead, Please. For the first time in my life I had to financially take care of things like gas for the car, insurance, and all of the stupid things I thought I needed as a teenager.* My job at the bead store was to help customers, clean things up, organize beads, brainstorm projects with local artists, put on kids' birthday parties, and help customers check out when they were ready to pay.

I loved all of that. It was the perfect first job. But I was so nervous on my first day. My hands were sweating, and I was afraid there was too much for me to remember. I fumbled through learning how to make jewelry out of a few beads and some wire, not to mention running a cash register for the first time. I remember thinking, *I am out of my league. I don't think I'll ever be able to do all this.*

Then, slowly but surely, I got used to how the shop worked and how to better serve the customers. Eventually, I was able to run that store alone. But those first-day nerves would return again and again as I moved to new jobs and new responsibilities. On my first day working at the University of Phoenix, taking live phone calls with potential students while a manager listened in, I thought I was going to throw up, I was so nervous. And my first time talking to my literary agent on the phone, I almost cried out of fear.

Firsts are like that. Saying yes to an opportunity or something new is just like that. It's going to push you. It's going to teach you. But on the other side of that yes is a whole lot of opportunity for growth.

If you want to be a successful momtrepreneur, you must say more yes to the right things. Say yes to that opportunity to sit down with someone you admire for coffee. Say yes to speak about something you're passionate about. Say *yes* to that person hoping to feature your product even if that yes means stepping out of your comfort zone.

Say yes in the space where you have time to learn. And if you don't have the time, make the time. Take stock of your priorities. List the things you find yourself doing each day, and then allow some wiggle room in

....

* Like sixty-four-ounce Dr. Peppers from Circle K and Sears Portrait Studios photoshoots with friends. Necessities, obviously.

there to learn. And don't be afraid to push yourself a little. (We learn more through hands-on, sweaty, clammy, I-don't-know-if-I-can-do-this decisions than the ones we're really comfortable with.)

Most of all, keep saying yes to new ideas, new possibilities, new opportunities, new input.

Read books.

Attend conferences a few times a year.

Hang around people who will force you to up your game.

Seek out those who will coach you.

Run after the things that make you nervous.

Never. Ever. Stop. Keep learning if you intend to keep growing.

11

SUCCESS PHILOSOPHY #8:
UNDERSTAND YOUR WHY

Not long ago I was preparing for a leadership event I was putting on for one hundred of the top leaders in my organization. I had noticed that many of the women I worked with just couldn't put their finger on why they wanted something more for their lives. After all, that's a heavy question to answer, and it takes a lot of introspection and self-knowledge to be able to justify just one reason for your being—especially given how much space being a mom takes up in our lives.

I was flipping through videos trying to help these women connect with what it is that they love to do. I wanted them to find the intersection of their passions and their skills so that they can find true meaning in their careers. During my search, I came across a video by Rob Bell where he talked about *ikigai*.[1]

Ikigai, according to Bell, is a Japanese word meaning "that which gets you up in the morning" or "what we were born to do." It's the *why* that drives so much of what you do and want to do.

Lightbulbs and fireworks with a side of dance party erupted in my brain when I heard that definition. *That's it!* I thought. The thing that gets us up in the morning—that's what we should build a business on. That's what we should build a business *for*. That's the thing we can so easily get lost in because it fulfills such a deep part of our brains and our hearts.

Each person's ikigai will be a combination of four things: what we're great at, what we love, what the world needs, and what we can be paid for. It's unique to the individual, coming from deep down inside us. And there's no right or wrong about it, despite what the voices of our culture might say. It's our "thing," what floats our boat, the why behind what we care about and want to do. And it's what each of us must discover about ourselves to live and work at our best.

Here's where my culture and I probably part ways: my ikigai isn't raising my babies. I love my three girls more than anything else in my life. They've brought significance into my life in a way that no other thing can or has. But they are not what gets me out of bed in the morning.* What gets me up in the morning is my life's work—a combination of writing, reading, strategizing, teaching, and speaking about women's entrepreneurship. That is what energizes me so deeply that, once I get started, my husband basically has to have an emergency shut-off button to get me to stop. My inability to stop working is the thing he and I fight about the most. When I'm not doing it, I'm thinking about it because I truly love what I do.

Women's entrepreneurship is my ikigai. It's the place where my passions and talents meet. It's also where I can provide for people who need it and can get paid to do it. My ikigai encompasses my passion, mission, profession, and vocation—as the diagram on page 173 shows. Yours will do the same.

What Is Your Ikigai?

Before you settle on what your ikigai is, I want to remind you that it's not based around the happiness or love of another person. As moms, I find we have a tendency to make our important thoughts, actions, and decisions

---

* Well, they do get me up every morning, but I don't do it with a smile. My husband warns them every morning, "Don't poke the bear."

about someone else because that's what we're used to and that's what is socially acceptable. We can so easily tell people that everything we do is about our kids. I do it all the time, but it's not necessarily true. For some moms, nurturing children can be their ikigai. But that doesn't have to be true for every mom.

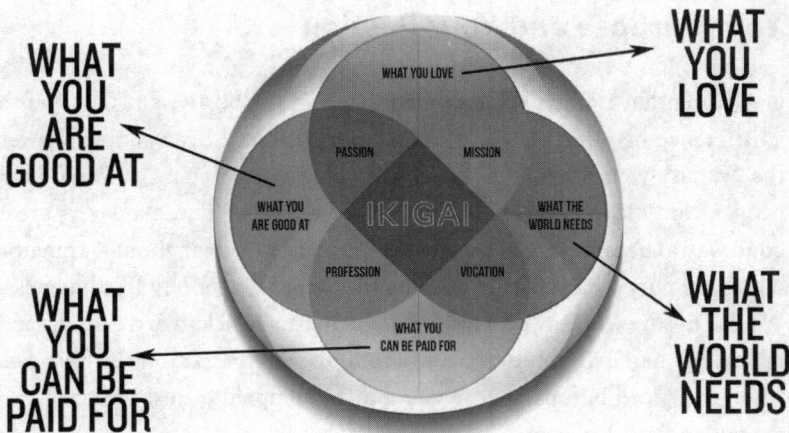

WHAT YOU ARE GOOD AT

WHAT YOU LOVE

WHAT YOU CAN BE PAID FOR

WHAT THE WORLD NEEDS

WHAT YOU LOVE

PASSION

MISSION

WHAT YOU ARE GOOD AT

IKIGAI

WHAT THE WORLD NEEDS

PROFESSION

VOCATION

WHAT YOU CAN BE PAID FOR

Ladies, your ikigai is yours alone, and your business can be totally about you. Don't you dare feel shame about that. Loving what you do as a career doesn't make you a subpar mom. It just makes you a more productive and fulfilled one.

I have to tell you it took me awhile to know myself well enough to recognize my ikigai. I knew I was drawn to the idea of entrepreneurship, and I found myself starting businesses in my twenties without examining why I wasn't doing what all of my friends were doing. They were all out there in the workforce, throwing around the college diplomas, trying to climb the corporate ladder while I was doing freelance scrapbooking. When that didn't work I tried the predictable path—corporate job, marriage, children. Even when I fell backward into my first million-dollar-producing business, the light hadn't dawned yet. I had been through enough life to know a bit about why I was making the choices I was. But I still wasn't fully aware of what was driving my choices—and that's shaky ground to build a business on.

Self-knowledge and self-discovery, in other words, usually develop slowly, over a period of years. So be patient with yourself as you try to figure out what you were born to do and the whys that drive you. It will come, and if you're like me, it will change you.

Your Purpose and Your Passion

One thing that I didn't realize when I started my business is that there's a difference between purpose and passion. Often, I hear people answer the "What's your why?" question by stating their passion: "I love to help people," or "I love to create things with my hands." Those answers are a good way to become one of those starving artists we hear about—a creator without a purpose can easily become the owner of a hobby-like business. While I'm sure working on a hobby is a lot of fun, it lacks a drive to succeed or make a mark. If you don't connect your passion to a bigger purpose, when the speed bumps appear you may be tempted to just park the car, get out, and walk away.

I have a friend who has a passion for being creative and connecting with other people. The problem is that there's no purpose for her to do those things outside of the fact that she just likes it. There's no goal or driving reason for her to work with excellence and to keep working even when things get tough. The chances that she simply walks away from her passions are high because she's missing that deeper sense of purpose of her actions.

Her purpose could be to use her talents and skills and, yes, passion to grow a business that allows her to pay for her kids' college on her own. Maybe it's so she can take the trips she's always dreamed of with her family. Without purpose, passion easily falls flat in the face of adversity.

I think this is the exact reason we see so many wannabe entrepreneurs hop from shiny thing to shiny thing without the growth and stamina needed to sustain a business through the rough patches. In order to find a course and stick with it to the point of being successful, they need a better grasp of how their passion and their purpose can come together.

They need to understand their ikigai.

Finding Your Ikigai

Still not smacked in the face with what it is that gets you out of bed in the morning? That's okay, you're totally normal. Most people are in your same boat. Here are a few questions that may help you brainstorm how to find your why and connect your passion with your purpose.

I usually find that the best way for me to work through something like this is to talk it out with someone who is close to me and knows me well. Another way is to journal in a stream-of-consciousness style. Try one of those techniques for answering the questions below. Don't worry about formal grammar or punctuation. Just start writing. Keep peeling back the layers.

Start by answering these three questions:

- What do you do?
- How do you do it?
- Why do you do it?

From there let's dig a little bit deeper:

- Can you identify who you are outside of typical roles in your life? Who are you outside of being a mom, a wife, an employee, a daughter, or a friend?
- What happened that finally made you say yes to your business?
- What makes you excited about your business?
- What is the goal of your business?
- How will you feel when you reach your goal?
- What does success look like to you in your business?
- If you were to fail, how would you feel?
- What's the point of growing your business?
- What do you want your legacy to be?

My hope is that you'll keep asking yourself why questions until you start to feel emotional. When I started to cry, I knew I had hit the nail on the head. You should absolutely be emotionally connected to why you're sacrificing so much to grow a dream. Keep asking questions until you feel the tears sting your eyes. That's when you'll know you've discovered your ikigai.

As I've mentioned, my ikigai is encouraging and enabling women's entrepreneurship. I want to change the way women think about the possibilities of owning their own businesses, and I want to be a part of changing the culture to make entrepreneurship a real, viable, and exciting choice.

These days everything I do, as far as work is concerned, connects directly to that thing that gets me up in the morning. I know it's going to take a lot of work and dedication. But I'm willing to do it because it's the thing I think about every single day. I believe it's part of my purpose, my why. I believe God gave me certain skills and desires just so I can impact women through business ownership and leadership.

My friend Ali Edwards is a designer, writer, and momtrepreneur who has a passion for the place where stories and pictures connect. I've seen her build an incredible business and tribe that allows her to help women tell their everyday stories, the stories we often believe are insignificant or uninteresting. Her purpose is to create products—journals, workbooks, scrapbooking supplies, inspirational materials—that inspire women to capture and share their stories in new and creative ways. This in turn allows them to leave a legacy for their kids, remember small details in their everyday lives, and connect with those they care about on a deeper level.

Ali's been able to provide for her family by doing exactly what she loves and believes is important. She encourages women by telling her own story in a very real way, the struggles as well as the highlights. Ali's passion, purpose, and business always reminds me of what's really important in life and allows me to live my version of the good life because she was willing to see the importance of storytelling and what she calls memory keeping. She's a great example of the power of ikigai.

So are you ready to name your own ikigai? It's okay if you aren't—you'll get there. But if it's beginning to come together in your mind, I want you to go ahead and write it down. Think through what we've discussed in the last few pages and put down your best answer to the fundamental question, "What gets you out of bed in the morning?"*

_____

_____

_____

_____

_____

Sharing Your Ikigai

It's not enough to know why you're starting your business. Now you have to share it, which for some is even more difficult. It may require being brave enough to be vulnerable with your customers or employees or team members. The more clearly you can explain why your business exists, the easier it will be to gain buy-in and trust from others. That buy-in and trust will propel you toward your goals and make saying yes so much easier for your customers.

Understanding why you're doing what you do and sharing that understanding makes such a difference. It keeps you connected to a deeper meaning in your life and helps you move through challenges. We all have a desire to be inspired and to be a part of something that's bigger than we are. We love to make things happen, to make a difference with our lives. That's part of what makes humans so special. And it's a big part of what makes sharing your ikigai so powerful. Sharing your why can help inspire the people who follow you. It gives them something to believe in and re-iterates the truth:

....

* Another similar question is: "What righteously pisses you off?" Whichever works for you.

I like you.
You like me.
We are alike.
We are a tribe.

This truth will build a tribe around you, and that tribe will help insulate you from the bad days and things that people outside your tribe will say about you. Having people who love and support you is integral to success in your business and your life. You cannot do it without the help of other people.

You have to go first though. You have to identify why you're choosing this business at this time and then share that why with everyone. Your heart should be one of the first things people see when it comes to your business.

If that scares you, I get it. It scares me too. I naturally tend to keep all the soft spaces in my heart hidden behind a steel wall where I can't be hurt.* That's not my lot in life though. If you want to play big, you have to risk big.

There is a group out there that is on your side. That's your tribe. They're waiting for you to show up for them and go all in. So do it. Tell the backstories that led you to believe what you do about your product or service. Talk about the hard things that you had to walk through to get to this place in your life in business. Don't worry if you get emotional when you talk about your connection to what you do. That's appropriate.

After all, you're doing what you were born for.

....

* And where things can fester and become a real problem in my life because I don't talk about them. Note to self: schedule appointment with psychologist.

12

SUCCESS PHILOSOPHY #9: TREAT YOUR BUSINESS LIKE A BUSINESS

Michael and I were audited by the state twice last year. Over the course of a few weeks, we received two notifications that our taxes were under investigation. Nothing will make you feel like you were just punched in the stomach like the word *audit*. But never have I been so grateful to realize I had taken the time to treat our business like a business—and get it set up so something like an audit is an annoyance, not a disaster.

When my business first started taking off, I realized really fast how unorganized I was and how realities such as receipts, taxes, and changes in the law tended to hit the back burner when I was in charge. I was busy worrying about other things. It was about six months in when I realized that (1) I needed to do this financial/legal thing right and (2) I was not qualified for the job. I just don't have the desire to sort through receipts and keep logs of every mile I drive. So I knew right then and there that I would have to hire someone to help me.

This was my version of treating my business like a business. I knew that if I wasn't willing to take on the back end of my business, someone would have to. I couldn't ignore it forever. So I hired a really good accountant and I convinced my husband* to leave his job and come help me run this fledgling business.

If I had continued to ignore the parts of my business that kept it running but that I didn't love, my business would have gone under. I would probably be in jail because paying bills is not my forte.** That's what Michael is great at doing. I'm the wow; he's the how. It works for us.

I think that many momtrepreners struggle to treat businesses as a serious, important part of our lives. It's not just a hobby. We aren't doing it out of the goodness of our hearts. We have a desire to take our products or services and make them profitable. Your business isn't just something you do. It's deeply important to you. You need to own that fact.

I've met so many women who shrug off their business ventures like it's a silly little thing they do to pass the time instead of a legitimate endeavor. Sometimes I wonder if they're ashamed of what they do, especially when their businesses are not yet fully established. Would you be embarrassed if you worked a corporate gig? Would you be able to shrug off a job if you got paid an hourly rate and had to put on pants to do it? I'd venture to say no.

I think we should feel the same about your at-home businesses. Just because you can work around spilled bowls of Cheerios while going an unhealthy amount of time without a shower doesn't make your job any less real.

It's real.

It's yours.

Own it.***

Money

Money can be super awkward to talk about. I find women in particular have a really hard time discussing money, and I think that just comes from

....

* After many sexual favors and long talks about stability.

** It doesn't matter how much money is in the bank account. I will always forget to put a check in the mail or fill out paperwork on time.

*** Also own the no-pants days because they are one of the best perks of working at home. You're welcome.

being new to business. But the more their business becomes a regular part of their lives, the more they realize just how important money is to a momtrepreneur.

I also think many people have it in their head that working to make money is somehow not a noble thing to do—that if we are working to make money to be able to live a different kind of life, we're doing something bad. But it wouldn't be bad if we were drawing a regular paycheck from a corporate gig, right? Why is this different?

Let me be super clear: making money is the point of owning a business. Otherwise we'd just call it a hobby.

It's okay to want to make money in your business. It's okay to want to make a crazy amount of money in your business. Money is not inherently good or bad. Only when we make money the most important thing does it become a bad thing. As my favorite pastor, Scott Nickel, puts it, "When a good thing becomes an ultimate thing, ultimately that good thing becomes a very bad thing." That is true of money.

You had this idea for a business because you wanted to meet needs, help people, and build a rewarding career for yourself. You want to have the ability to say yes to anything you feel is important and necessary in your life. That costs money, and that's okay.

Making money is a good thing. It will provide you with an ability to do amazing things for you, for your family, and for others. It will buy you more yes in your life.

My number-one rule when it comes to money in business is to make sure you pay yourself. You must pay yourself for your time. You don't have to give yourself a full salary at first if your business can't quite afford you, but you need to take *something* for yourself. Don't be that girl who stands up in front of people and pats herself on the back for never having taken a dime of money from her business. That's not noble. That's a terrible business plan.

When Michael and I agreed that I would do my best to make my business work, we set parameters around money. I had to make enough to make the time away from our family worth it. If it wasn't doing that, I was willing to walk away from it after a few years. Then later, when it was time for Michael to quit his nine-to-five job, we set a certain financial goal that we had to hit for us to make that happen.

Never forget that making money is the first purpose of having a business. You're not doing what you do for self-expression or home-office deductions or doing good though those elements may be a factor in your work. But you have to have an eye for the bottom line, or you're not going to have a business for long.

Lawyers and Contracts and Taxes! Oh My!

Another crucial part of being a business owner who actually stays in business is taking the time to handle your finances and properly protect yourself and your business from future storms. If you're anything like me, you're going to need a team of good people around to help you. The following sections detail just a few things you will want to think about as you're building your business. You can't afford not to think about them.

Taxes, Accountants, and Bookkeepers

Of the many things I'm good at, paying bills on time is not one of them. I forget to do it.

Let me explain to you a little bit about how my brain works. I can have a meeting on my calendar, and I can see that reminder in the morning and again an hour before it's supposed to start. But if I get into my work flow between the time I saw that reminder and when the meeting starts, I'll completely space out on the meeting. When my brain really gets into actually working, I forget absolutely everything else. My employees and my husband now know to remind me when something is on the calendar no fewer than seven times in the final hour before I need to be there because they know me. They know I'll space it, and then I'll get mad at myself.

So, yeah, paying quarterly taxes and organizing my receipts isn't something I'm great at, but for someone who owns a business, it's a job requirement. So I went and hired my husband away from his job in corporate America to help me by running the entire back end of my (now our) business. I think it was extremely clever of me to marry a man way back then who was qualified to do this.

If you don't have a Michael waiting in the wings to help you with taxes and all the intricacies of business ownership, you'll have to learn how to do it yourself or find a professional to help you—perhaps a little of both. Actually, even if you do have a Michael, I recommend finding a pro. Hire an accountant or CPA you really trust to do your taxes and help you make sure you're saving yourself as much money as possible and you're writing off all the right expenses. Put a plan in place to make sure you're abiding by the law and helping yourself succeed at the same time.

Even if you're working with a pro, it doesn't hurt to educate yourself about the business of having a business. There are some great books out there that can help you understand what you can and can't write off. *475 Tax Deductions for Businesses and Self-Employed Individuals* by Bernard B. Kamoroff helped me a lot when I first started dealing with tax stuff.[1] Ask your accountant which resources would be best to help you make good choices throughout the year before you hand your numbers over to him or her.

Michael and I have the best accountant in the world. His name is Patrick, and he's been an integral part of our business from the beginning, before Michael and I had two pennies to rub together.* Patrick has similar values and beliefs for his life and work as Michael and I do for ours. We absolutely love working with Patrick and the people in his office, and I think Patrick loves our story of going from nothing to millions. I hope he never retires.

As our business grew, Michael and I hired one of Patrick's staff members to do our bookkeeping so we could keep all our financial activities in one place. Patrick knows about all of our side businesses, too, and his help has been immeasurable as we navigated these new waters.

As for our taxes—the man is a godsend. When we received those audit notices from the state, Patrick helped us figure out what the problem

....

* Patrick is a CPA, and he's also a marriage counselor because . . . money.

was, then went back through our past years' returns to make sure everything was right. When he found that there had been a miscalculation on his part, he called immediately and owned up to the mistake. And the very next week we opened an envelope to find a $16,000 check to make up for the money we owed the state. That man was prepared to pay our taxes, y'all.

Of course, we tore up that check. Patrick isn't responsible for our taxes, but he sure did solidify us as lifelong clients of his that day.

I hope you can find a CPA like that, one who is more concerned with people than the bottom line. Build a relationship with that person and let him or her guide you. It will make all the difference.

Contracts

As your business grows, you'll start to work with other people who have skill sets or time that you do not have. That's awesome. You can hire them to lessen some of your load. But when you start hiring help, you need to also think about contracts. Always have an agreement that lays out what you will pay and what they will do. Every detail should be in there so you both know what to expect in this business transaction.

Here's where you might be saying, "But it's my brother. I don't need a contract for him, do I?"

Yes, you do.

"But my friend is going to help me, and I feel weird about having her sign a contract. Do I still have to have one?"

Yes, you do.

And it's going to be uncomfortable; I can promise you that. You won't want to ask someone to sign a contract. You won't feel comfortable locking him or her into something with a signature because you'll feel that you should trust each other. You won't want to be the one who presents a document that seems to say "I don't fully trust you" to someone that you do, in fact, trust.

You won't want to, but because you've read this, you will get that contract signed. When you know better, you do better, right?

Always have a contract. Always. You can hire a lawyer to put one together. You can use online services like Rocket Lawyer or Legal Zoom. I don't care where the contract comes from. But before you exchange a penny or a minute with anyone who is going to work for you, you get that contract signed. Protect yourself, keep your business transactions clean, and then hope you never have to look at it or need it again.

You'll be amazed what some of the people you trust will do to grab a stack of your cash if it's easier than working. You might also be surprised at how easy it is for you to take advantage of people working for you. (A contract is for their protection too!) I've lost friends and family over that kind of thing, and I take the responsibility for not getting a contract up front. The whole purpose of the contract is to preserve the relationship, not to hurt it.

Say no to kale and beet salad. Don't say no to contracts.

Lawyers

You don't necessarily need a lawyer on retainer when you first start your business. As your business grows, though, you'll probably have a need for one.

Michael and I first retained a lawyer to help us draw up a will and trust for our family. Currently only 42 percent of Americans have a will set up. That means that over half of Americans have no plans for what to do with themselves, their money, and their possessions if they die.

It's not fun to think about what happens when you or your partner dies, but I can promise you that having no plan is one of the worst mistakes you can make. It leaves so much unknown and so much work on the person left alive in that situation.

Don't give your kids or family members a reason to fight over you when you're not there anymore. Lay out exactly what you want done with your money and possessions if you pass away. Get yourself a will and a trust so that you can protect your assets. It won't take you longer than an afternoon to answer some super awkward questions with your spouse about when you'd like them to pull the plug. And it won't cost you an arm and a leg. I promise you, you need it.

Go find an estate-planning lawyer and draw up your will and trust.

Make a plan for what would happen to your business if something should happen to you. Think it all through and put it on paper.

Investments

Once you are fully responsible to bring in money for your business and your family, you are also responsible to plan for your future. Your retirement isn't going to build itself. It's up to you to build it. Here, again, we have a subject that I am not a professional in. I know a little, but not enough to deal with something as large as what Michael and I plan to have when we retire. I suggest you find a financial planning group or an investment banker to help you decide the right place for your money to grow.

Our financial planners and our CPA have talked on more than one occasion to get on the same page. We are exploring all kinds of retirement vehicles to get to the place where we can travel the world together and have amazing experiences with our family.

Your first step should be to find a financial planner to help guide you.

Your next step is to get with your partner and start dreaming about what you want to do in your golden years.

Insurance

A great insurance agent who will return your phone calls promptly and take care of you when you need it is worth his or her weight in gold. You probably already have insurance for your home, auto, life, and health, but you'll need to think about insurance for your business well. Your current insurance agency may be able to help you with this, or they may direct you to another company.

Find out what options you have and protect your business by getting insurance to cover any assets you acquire—equipment, autos, storage buildings, offices, and so on—and any incidents that may occur. This is especially true if you put on events or may ever be in a situation where someone might decide to sue you. Prepare for the worst and expect the best. You got this.

Partnership with Your Spouse

When I first started my at-home business, my husband worked a more-than-full-time corporate gig in Seattle. He'd come home at the end of the day, and I swear the look of sheer horror on his face when he'd walk through the door was priceless. The girls would likely be playing with knives and contraband in the living room and eating their Happy Meals while I shoved a cheeseburger (no pickles, please) into my face and stared into my computer.

I'm not saying I did this thing right, people. I didn't. I wasn't prepared for how much work entrepreneurship was going to take, but I knew I was lost in it and I loved it. I loved it so much that I was willing to sacrifice almost all my time for it. I hadn't gotten real with myself about how this was all going to work, and I hadn't sat down and had a conversation about it with my husband.

I'm not going to lie to you—Michael and I could come in first and second place in the stubborn Olympics.* This creates some epic battles between us, and the battles we had during the time I was starting my business were ones for the record books. He wanted everything back to the way it was before I "worked." (Do those intentional quotation marks make your blood boil too?) I wanted to be able to contribute financially to the family and use my brain for something outside of playing Barbie—with a nude doll—and a permanent bad-hair day.

For the next few months we fought about this, and each of us was frustrated with the other for not understanding how we felt. Michael would make fun of me, I would get super angry at him, and then we would play

....

* I mean, I'd win, obviously, but I'll give him second place because I'm a giver like that.

an epic round of the quiet game, just the two of us. We just weren't connecting because we disagreed about a fundamental part of our relationship and our family dynamic.

Honestly, looking back, I should have been a more understanding wife. After all, I was the one who had changed my mind about being a stay-at-home mom to our three girls. But he wasn't giving an inch, either. So we were sort of at an impasse.

Fast forward six months—when I said we were stubborn, I meant it—and we finally sat down in a neutral time and place to actually discuss this thing we had going on.

Michael admitted that my starting a business had made him feel like he wasn't doing a good job providing. Hearing this made me feel sad because that wasn't my reason for starting my business at all. I admitted that I wasn't fulfilled staying home with the kids all day and that I avoided playdates like the black plague. (More kids? Are you out of your freaking mind?) Hearing that made Michael feel sad because my business was consuming my waking hours, and he worried that the kids and the house were being neglected. Then we both cried because we truly do love each other and want the best for each other. We had just been terrible communicators, and the more we fought, the worse it had gotten.

We came to a compromise where he would take over the kids when he got home from work, and I would do family breakfast on Saturday mornings without work or a phone. He gave me the space to treat my work like a legit business, and I got a better sense of what he needed from me as a mom and a wife. Our new arrangement worked until a year or so later, when I was able to convince Michael to quit his job and work with me. Thank God he said yes. I couldn't have managed without Michael's support.*

The same is likely true for your marriage. You have to talk to your

....

* And to this day I still can't. I've realized that if something happened to my husband, I wouldn't even know how to get in our house because I don't have a key. He does it all, and he's always there.

spouse. It's a major step in being able to own the word *entrepreneur*. You simply can't put in the effort required without support, especially the support of your spouse. Your partner can make or break your business success, so it's worth it to try to talk through your issues. Go find a counselor to mediate the conversation if you need to, but you both need to explain how you're feeling and what you want from your life, especially if it's changed.

All of this applies primarily to married women with kids, of course. If you're a single mom—or just single—you'll have a different set of dynamics. A lot of the same principles apply to working things out with older kids, other household members, ex-spouses, and friends.

In the previous section we talked about your ikigai. If spouses or partners don't know what gets you out of bed in the morning, now is the time to share it. Just open up. Let yourself be vulnerable. Feel your feelings and communicate them clearly. Ask spouses or partners for their support, just as you want to support their careers. Share your vision for your company and where you think your vision can take you. Let them know why you'd even want that.

It's almost inevitable that your business will change parts of the way you work together, and it could create a shift in priorities. That can be difficult to navigate. But do your best to keep the love and the communication alive and open.

If partners are the breadwinners in the family and this role is important to them, it is really important that you do not frame your entrepreneurial desires in terms that might belittle their contributions. Imagine how defensive you'd become if someone called the way you parent your children into question. Don't make your spouses or partners feel that you're picking up the slack because they haven't done enough.

By the same token, you are an equal member of the family, and it is okay for you to want something else and to go after your dreams. Your career is no less important than your spouse's or partner's career, even when it isn't paying the bills (yet). Be bold enough to ask for what you want and have reasons that will back you up.

PRO TIP

I find that most women who arm themselves with numbers and facts have a lot of success when they talk to their partners about their business. If your partner is at all analytical, you don't want to show up to the communication party without a few facts and figures. I literally took the time to do a bunch of math on the back of a napkin to show Michael just how much I thought my business would be able to bring in for us. I then told him honestly how I was feeling and what I needed from him. That was our turning point. Facts and feelings combined can't miss.

Feel the Fear, and Do it Anyway

Most of us care about what others think about us. It's why the idea of stepping out to create a new business freaks out a lot of people.

At some point after you step out with your own business, the negativity will come. Shockingly, it may come from the people closest to you. Little jokes here and there, an eye roll, a side comment to mutual friends or family—I've heard it all, and all of it hurts.

That's when the fear starts to creep into your thoughts about your business. It's not just excitement mixed with fear anymore. It's more than that. Sometimes I think I can physically feel the fear as it takes over; it starts at my toes and creeps all the way up until I'm covered in it.

I have a cousin, Adam, who is a brilliant businessman and inventor.* He's a great mix of a creative and a doer. He's had a lot of different businesses during his career, but right now he's focused on growing his great new company, Plank & Mill, which creates reclaimed wood planks with adhesive backing for use in DIY home projects.

....

* I'm really hoping this entrepreneurial Teague gene passes down to my kids too.

I've watched Adam build each one of his businesses with determination, strategy, and lots of hours. Yet I once heard another member of our family say, "Adam will do anything to avoid getting a real job." I remember looking over at my husband, and my eyes were surely bugging out of my head.

Adam laughed about it because, duh, entrepreneurs are the brand of crazy that will work a hundred hours a week as long as they can avoid that dreaded forty-hour work week. But it was then I realized that entrepreneurship scares people. They smack it down through little jokes and comments because they're afraid of what building our dreams says about them working a traditional nine-to-five. We are entrepreneur-ing at them. Right?

The truth is Adam has worked extremely hard all his adult life. He's traveled around to get his product in front of people. He's taken risks. He's paid his dues. He's failed. He's won. He's put everything on the line to build his dream. In other words, entrepreneurship is a real job—as long as you take it that seriously and you work your business hard. Nobody's snide comment can change that.

I've since learned a little bit about how our brains work, and this knowledge has allowed me a little more grace for people who want to make fun of what we do. You see, we are still the same kind of social animals we were back when we lived in caves. How does a caveman survive? In a pack, of course. If there are eight people in your pack, your chances against that bear over there are a lot higher than if it's just Frank out there alone with his spear and the bear. Frank needs people to survive.

So what happens when one of our pack starts to wander off? We yell, we scream, we shame, we do anything we can to pull that person with the crazy ideas back into the fold. Somewhere buried deep in our brains is the notion that we need that person with us if we are going to survive. *Come on, Kristin—the bear is right over there, and we need you with us, not wandering off to sell widgets.*

The thing is our environment has changed. Unless you are a character on any one of the thousands of reality TV shows about Alaska,* you don't

....

* And my husband watches Every. Single. One. God love him.

have to worry about a giant grizzly eating you for lunch. But even though our circumstances are different, our brains haven't changed that much. *Go get Kristin; she's about to leave us vulnerable. Hit her where it hurts so she will take up her proper role in our pack.*

You may notice that your friends do this to you. If all of them are stay-at-home moms and you start having ideas about starting a business, you'll probably hear about it, and not in a good way. Your girlfriends don't realize their brain is tricking them into feeling some negative, fearful emotions our species once needed for survival. Their brains think there is danger lurking, and before they even examine why they feel scared about your choices for your life, they try to pull you back down to "normal." It's natural. It's how we were designed. Our environment has evolved; our brains have not.

Now that you know this, you can do better when you're in the pack and another member starts to have new ideas that threaten the strength of the group. You don't need to pull them back down to normal because you are not in danger—and she is not making choices at you. Support her. Love her. Tell her you are her biggest fan.

Unfortunately, when you're the one whose entrepreneurial ambitions are being perceived as a threat, there's not too much you can do except bear with it and persist. You're going to have to want your business more than you care about what your neighbor thinks about your business. Even worse, you may have to want it more than you care about what your aunt says every single time you see her at a family gathering.

You're going to have to have hard conversations with the people you care about. Explain how the little actions and comments make you feel and ask for support even if they don't like the product or service you're offering or the fact that you now have a business. I think you'll find that most of them will do as you ask because you're important to them. They don't have to sell out your T-shirt shop, but they should stop with the snide, hurtful comments. If they're not willing to do that, is your friendship really worth saving? Is it worth spending extra time with them? Try to keep in mind that their negativity isn't about you; it's about them. Don't let them derail what you believe in.

Meanwhile, you may find that your family and friends are not the only ones who are fearful about your new venture. The business itself may stir up fears in you that you didn't know were there or haven't thought about in years and bring them to the surface, where it feels like everyone else can see them.

In March 2015, two years after I started my essential oils business, I decided to cut back a little on my working time, and I found myself wrestling with surprising emotions. I actually had to go to counseling to talk through my fear of losing my identity as a leader and of not being enough, doing enough, and being perfect for the people I worked with.[*]

I was a true hot mess at that time, but the counseling helped. While I didn't walk away magically cured of all my fears, I did become more equipped to handle them and to know which ones were real and which were just old tapes I was playing over and over in my head. I'm a firm believer that we've all got a little cuckoo going on upstairs and working through it with a professional can be beneficial for both your life and your business.

I've also tackled many of my fears through reading books. And the greatest advice I've ever been given about dealing with fear is to get it out of my head and onto paper—physically write it down—or speak it out loud. If you can do that, it becomes a lot less scary.

When I was a little kid, I went through a time when I was obsessed with the idea that I'd be kidnapped and sent to some creeper carnie family during the night. Not surprisingly, this messed-up fear kept me up at night in terror. But then the next morning, in the light of day, I'd wonder why I had been so scared about it. *Carnies aren't even real . . . right?*[**] That's kind of how I feel today when I write down my fears or say them out loud. I almost feel stupid saying some of them because I can tell how far from the truth they really are.

Sometimes I use my social media feed to bounce my fears around and

....

[*] There's no shame in my game. I'd go, talk like a crazy person for an hour, and then I'd sit in my car for an hour afterward and cry. Every week. Like clockwork.
[**] Wink, wink.

get them out of my head. Simply explaining them to my tribe helps them realize we're alike and also helps me realize that I'm in charge of not letting my fear run my life.

When I watched the Internet destroy an author online one day, I got super scared. What if that happened to me? Then I took a couple of deep breaths and shared what I was feeling with my tribe on social media. By the next morning I was pumped up, prepared to face my fear, and ready for whatever the Internet decided to throw at me.

At this point in my career I've learned to use my fear as an indication that something might be a good idea for me. If I find myself afraid to do it, that's a good sign that I *should* do it. If I'm scared to write something I believe to be truthful, for instance, I take that fear of rejection or nasty online pushback and use it as motivation to write it anyway.

I've found that some of the best things that have happened in my business came from working through fear. I feel so good about my workday when I can walk through something that's scary. Every time I do, it gets easier. And I care a little less about what people think.

I hope that some of these strategies will work for you too. Try feeling the fear, naming it, owning it as yours, and then go ahead and do what you were going to anyway. If it sticks around or recurs, try talking about it with a friend or, better yet, a counselor.

The process of working through your fears probably won't feel good. It might even hurt. But it's going to be worth it. This is one very hard part of business ownership; the what-ifs and the negative self-talk are hard to combat. But if you're willing, working through it all can change your life.

If you let it, your business will stretch you in every possible way and you'll come out the other side a more wholehearted and confident person. Plan on owning every part of your business and letting it work for you for the rest of your life.

13

SUCCESS PHILOSOPHY #10: SET GOALS + WORK HARD + REFUSE TO FAIL

Friends, have you been to an Ed Sheeran concert? He just walks out in front of an entire stadium full of people, pulls out his guitar, hits a few buttons on his foot pedal, and goes to town. Alone. With no band behind him. It's my guess that he gave zero effs about his hair or what he was wearing. And he lays down a concert that's so good you wouldn't believe it.*

I recently listened to an interview with Sheeran in which he talked about his days of grinding out his music in bars, playing in smoke-filled rooms just to make enough money to get to the next gig. But even during those early days, Sheeran's goals were never exactly small. "Two years ago, I said I want to play at Wembley Stadium in London. This year, I am doing it three times. It's when you say it out loud, people think you are crazy. But you can't care. The worst thing you can do is get halfway to that and then leave."[1]

Sheeran never gave himself the option of a Plan B. Instead, he set goals,

....

* Me and the teenyboppers—Sheeran fans for life.

worked hard, and refused to fail—exactly what we're going to dive into deeper in this chapter.

Now this is where I should give notice: I'm going to get a little rough with you here. We've covered nine success philosophies together, and you're well on your way to bossing up now. You're ready for me to share some hard truths that may cause you to bristle a bit but can make all the difference in getting you where you want to be.

Be S.M.A.R.T. About Setting Goals

Setting and demolishing goals is one of my favorite things in life. I live for setting ridiculous goals and then somehow, by the grace of God, finding a way to meet them.

In 2005, I attended a real estate conference with my mom. (I was working as her transaction coordinator and marketing department at the time.) At that conference, I had the great pleasure of hearing entrepreneur and author Jim Rohn talk about goal setting. What he said that day changed my life.

Because of that day I began setting goals in six different areas in my life: personal, spiritual, financial, health, business, and relationships. I set five-year (long-term) and one-year (short-term) goals that connect to each other. I find that this practice helps me take smaller, more bite-sized steps toward my ultimate long-term goals. Those smaller steps keep me moving and keep the goal fresh in my mind.

Read any number of self-help or business books, and clearly there is incredible power in goal setting. If we're really honest with ourselves, though, setting real goals in all areas of our lives can be a little scary and a little intimidating. It requires clearing out the cobwebs in some dark corners of life and some serious soul searching about what makes us happy, what we want in our short life here on earth, and what is truly important to us. That thought process can lead us down the "shoulda, woulda, coulda" path pretty easily. To top it off, while being honest about our past mistakes can be a great learning opportunity, it can also trigger negativity, which is the thief of joy. We must recognize the difference between taking an honest look at our life path and wallowing in regret and self-loathing.

If you're willing, however, I'd like to suggest that we go ahead and shine that light in some dark corners and clean up our lives the best we can, and I suggest we create a space in our businesses to do the same. We must actively pursue significance in all areas of our lives in order to call ourselves successful.

We all want success, right? Well, let's run after it then—not just in business, but in our personal and spiritual lives, in our finances, and within our families. And the most dependable tool we have for achieving success is to set—you guessed it—measurable, written goals. Post a copy of goals on your bathroom mirror or on your wall where you can see them daily. Share them with your spouse and friends. Put a reminder on your phone. Do everything you can to review them every single day.

After a lot of practice in goal setting, I've come to believe that setting S.M.A.R.T. goals in three different stages (long-term, short-term, and daily action items) is the best way to achieve them. Every goal you write from now on should meet the following criteria—and while you may have heard of S.M.A.R.T. goals, let's review anyway. We're talking about goals that are

- Specific,
- Measurable,
- Achievable,
- Relevant, and
- Timely.

Do you see the difference? An ordinary goal might be: "I want to read more." A S.M.A.R.T. goal would be: "I make time each night to read for fifteen minutes without distraction or guilt."

Goals for the Long Term

To get the most out of setting goals and to give us the best chances of success, we need to follow a precise path—and setting long-term goals first is the best way to start down that path. Think to yourself, *Where do I want to be in five years?* Then write your long-term goals below (remember the S.M.A.R.T. criteria):

1. **Personal.** What are the things you've always wanted to do for yourself? What do you feel the desire to accomplish personally in the next five or ten years? This section is just for you, and there aren't right or wrong answers. (Don't write personal goals for others, such as your partner or children.)

_____

_____

_____

2. **Spiritual.** Take a good, hard look at your spiritual life. What might be improved by simply spending more time focusing on what you believe? Spiritually speaking, what do you struggle with that you feel a strong desire to explore further? What could you spend time doing to create a stronger connection to your faith?

_____

_____

_____

3. **Financial.** Money is often a really hard part of our lives to unpack and get on top of. It's no wonder it causes so many problems for us if we aren't careful. What programs could you take part in to get a hold on your finances? What do you wish you had the money to do right now? What could you do to make your money work for you now and in the future?

_____

_____

_____

4. **Health.** Health goals not written down with action steps are so easily forgotten and put aside. What activity do you like to do that would help

you accomplish your health and wellness goals? What assessments might help you get a better handle on your health? How could better health improve your life?

_____

_____

_____

5. **Business.** As entrepreneurs we set a lot of goals for our work. How can you think big picture about what you want for your business? What rewards would come from creating a profitable business? How much income do you want to bring in, and how do you get there?

_____

_____

_____

6. **Relationships.** Without people, our lives could be so empty. It's important to focus on nurturing our relationships with the people in our lives. Think about how you could create more connection to your kids, your spouse, and your friends. How can you show people how important they are to you?

_____

_____

_____

Goals for the Shorter Term

Now that we have *your* big, long-term goals down on paper, let's break these into smaller step goals. I find that writing two-step goals for each big goal is a huge advantage to breaking down something that feels really far off in the future. Step goals will help you focus on objectives that are more easily accomplished but that help you move toward your bigger goals. These short-term goals will need to be very concrete and specific—the more specific, the better—and they should have a definite timetable. A good way to stay on track with them is to make sure your step goals are still following the S.M.A.R.T. goal format.

1. Personal

1. _____
2. _____

2. Spiritual

1. _____
2. _____

3. Financial

1. _____
2. _____

4. Health

1. _____
2. _____

5. Business

1. _____
2. _____

6. Relationships

1. _____
2. _____

If you find that the methods you're taking to get to your goals are becoming something you hate, don't hesitate to change your mind. These are your goals, and this is your life, so you get to make the rules. I recently wrote a goal for myself to "write for two hours each day." It took me about three days to realize I hated this goal. Rather than simply torture myself on my journey toward being a writer, I changed the goal to make it more enjoyable for me. Instead of writing every single day, I make it a goal to write ten hours a week. That way I am not tied down to a schedule, and I can be flexible in how I schedule my week, knowing writing has to be a part of it somewhere.

Now you have a complete path for your goals. I suggest that you check in on these short- and long-term goals often—daily, if possible—to stay on track toward the things you want to accomplish in and with your one wild and crazy life.

A Word About *Balance*

This may surprise you, but I don't believe in balance. I don't believe that if you're kicking tail in the office and really grinding out your goals in that area, you're going to be crushing it in the other portions of your life. Similarly, if your family is in some kind of crisis—maybe your mom is in the hospital or a teenager is acting out—you might be letting things slide a little bit elsewhere.

When I was working my business hard—like really hard—I was the worst friend. I turned down every offer from my girlfriends in order to make sure I was spending the necessary time to grow my business. I missed church a lot. I wasn't the most attentive mother. I surely did not hit the gym like I should have.

Finding balance in our lives is tough, impossible even. We go through seasons in our lives where we need to focus on one area or another and give less attention to the others. Those things will ebb and flow. Sometimes you'll be thriving in one area, only to find you're barely hanging on in another. That's okay.

I suggest you write your goals for each area anyway because as your circumstances and situations change, you may shift your focus from one area of life to another. That's also okay.

Here's the thing to remember though. These are *your* goals. This is *your* life. What you want is okay. It's all okay. Be confident to want what you want out of your life and have the guts to go after it—or choose not to. Just don't let someone else's idea of *balance* create a situation where you're working your tail off to live up to some impossible standard. To me, that's a recipe for unhappiness bordering on depression. Don't do it to yourself. Just do the best you can and know that there will have to be some give in some areas of your life when you really focus on growing in another.

The Hard Truth About Hard Work

Do you ever get sucked into the rabbit hole that is the Internet?

Who am I kidding? Most of us can answer that question with a follow-up one: "Do you mean how many times a day do I get sucked into the rabbit hole?"

I feel you, sister. So today one link led to another link that led to another link, and I found myself reading a blog post from Jennie Allen, who quotes her husband as saying, "Men don't know what their dreams are and women know, they are just afraid."[2] Which was such a slow-clap moment for me.*

I think there are so many men who don't know their dreams. They go into a particular field at a young age and become golden-handcuffed to that industry. They can't let themselves dream because that could mean instability for their families, whom they believe they have to support.

A woman though? Usually it will take just a few minutes of conversation to land on what makes her tick. She'll tell you every last detail as her face lights up about something she loves. If you really get to know her, she might even tell you what she dreams about for her and her family. It's as if she's created this whole perfect scenario for what could be and tucked it away in this imaginary place in her mind—kind of like she did when she was a kid playing house.

A mom may preface the juicy part about her dreams with "outside of my family, of course," because that's standard mom operating procedure. Moving to action and sticking out a plan to realize that dream

....

* When I have slow-clap moments, I imagine myself face-to-face with these famous Internet people doing the most awkward, straight-out-of-*Hoosiers* slow clap. It's awesome.

and actually create that life she's imagined. That's another thing entirely because—again—fear.

But I think there's something beyond fear that holds us back—another piece to this "why don't you just go for it" puzzle for women. And this may be hard for some to hear, but I'm just going to come out and say it:

Based on what I observe in my business and in my own personal experience, we're often held back because of the hard work that entrepreneurship entails.

It's not that we're lazy—not most of us, anyway. It's just that we're already working really hard as a mom. Often the scheduling, shuttling, prepping, cleaning, and basic chores of a household fall mostly on the woman's plate. So maybe we're not ready to put in a ton of effort into our side businesses because we're just freaking exhausted.*

To a certain extent, even in this "liberated" age, I think women are also conditioned against knowing what a physical and mental grind feels like. For many of us, I believe there is a cultural mind-set that gets drilled into us from a young age—often unintentionally—that hard work is for the tough boys and that us pretty girls should be doing something that's softer around the edges.

For whatever reason, many women aren't geared toward the kind of work that entrepreneurship requires. It's not that they can't. It's that they're not prepared. We're about to get prepared, though, because part of working hard is reversing our tendency to self-sabotage and to play the victim. So, friends, grab your drink of choice and let's keep going.

No More Getting in Our Own Way

Let me get super honest with you. We've touched on taking ultimate responsibility for your business. We've talked about how hard it is when you're genuinely authentic with your audience and they use it against you.

....

* Just typing out "scheduling, prepping, and cleaning" made me want a glass of red wine and a nap.

There's a lot of unknowns about being an entrepreneur. But still, the only person who can hold you back from reaching your goals is you. You are likely the biggest roadblock to your own success.

I know that's true for me. I am absolutely the one that stands in the way of everything I want—

- I don't believe I'm worthy.
- I don't believe I can.
- I doubt my choices.
- I believe the old tapes of doubt in my head.
- I give in to my fear.
- I don't learn through my failure.
- I let my desire for acceptance mess up the risks I take.

Or any of the thousand other reasons I use against myself.

When I started building my network marketing business in 2013, my process and ideas seemed to disrupt the norms of the company I repped for. We were growing fast—like speed-of-light fast—and that scared people. It made others look at themselves and feel like they weren't measuring up. They didn't want me to surpass their success because I hadn't "paid my dues" yet. They didn't understand me and how I worked. They didn't take the time to get to know me. All they knew was that they didn't have access to what my team was doing and that what we were doing was something they hadn't seen before.

I heard it all:

"You can't build a business on social media."
"You'll never be successful in this business."
"We don't work the way you do."

The rumors and gossip about me were so intense. I was getting hate mail and calls from the corporate office to try to shut me down every single week. It started with the established leaders on other teams, and it developed from there.

Working hard to grow a business while being public enemy number one inside the organization was terrifying, and it was hurtful. It was one of the hardest things I've ever done in my life.

It's been years now since I was the new person throwing a monkey wrench into business as usual, so the complaints and the hate mail have slowed way down. At this point we've grown so large that most of the other leaders know we're here to stay. Even then, with the dust mostly settled, I'm wary of being in a room with other leaders in the organization. I pull back. I retreat inward. I keep to myself. I avoid conversations. I become quiet. I worry constantly. All because I remember the things those leaders said about me and how they tried to hurt me and my business. I don't want to go through that again.

This is the hard part of being the industry disruptor. Something inside keeps telling me that even after all of these years, the other leaders on other teams hate me and what I stand for.

I know in my head that probably isn't true. I've even had a few co-workers sit me down and tell me the hard thing, which is that most people in the organization don't actually hate me. They may have had a problem with me in the beginning, but that was more about them than me and it's now in the past, not the present.

I hate to admit it, but they're probably right.

There are likely still some leaders within the organization who hold on to their negative feelings about me—and there's nothing I can do about. My belief that the other leaders hate everything about me is *my* problem now. I'm perpetuating that drama.

No one else.

Me.

I am in my own way in this situation. I could reach out and build relationships with other leaders in that company, but I hold myself back out of fear. It's just one example of the ways I get in the way of achieving my goals and reaching my full potential. And I think it's pretty safe to say I'm not alone in doing this sort of thing.

I want you to think about your business honestly and actually write down a few of the ways you hold yourself back from reaching your potential. What do you do to sabotage your own success? (Some possibilities are procrastination, doubt, worry, anger, low self-worth, low self-belief, or closed off communication.) Getting these self-sabotaging thoughts, feelings, and actions down on paper will help you be more aware of them and recognize them more quickly when you fall into old habits of pulling yourself away from your goals.

PRO TIP

One good way I've found to figure out if I'm standing in my own way is to ask myself, *Is what I believe a fact, or is it a thought?*

I am married to my husband. That's a fact.

There are days he wishes he didn't marry me. That's a thought.

If I act on that thought as a fact, I'm the problem. What I need to do is work through that thought by communicating or by letting my husband tell me if something is true or not.

With this in mind, list five ways you tend to self-sabotage and end up hurting your business:

_____

_____

_____

_____

_____

Self-sabotage can be a pernicious habit, but habits can be broken. Here are some helpful strategies for overcoming self-sabotage:

1. **Recognize the self-sabotaging pattern of behavior.** Ask yourself questions about why you're putting things off or not accomplishing your goals. Why do you find yourself breaking the promises you made to yourself?

2. **Take notice when you start to fall into negative thoughts or feelings about yourself.** It might be helpful to write down these thoughts and feelings into a journal while you're feeling them. Putting them on paper can help get them out of your head and keep you from dwelling on them.

3. **Ask yourself,** *Is what I believe a fact, or is it a thought?* If it is not a fact backed up by data, you need to challenge your negative thoughts or feelings about yourself.

4. **Remember to peel back the layers.** What is going on behind this negative thought or feeling about yourself or this self-sabotaging behavior? Where does it stem from? What past hurt are you protecting yourself from?

5. **Ask for feedback.** It's always a good idea to identify the "truth people" in your life. Truth people tell you their true opinions when you ask for them. Ask the people you love, that love you in return, for their opinions on your actions or thoughts. Give them permission to tell you if they see you self sabotaging.

6. **Encourage yourself.** Prove your thought wrong by coming up with an affirming statement. Write that statement on your mirror in your bathroom and say it out loud to yourself while you look yourself in the eyes every day. This may sound a little crazy, and you may not want to do this while other people are around.* But try it anyway. Positive affirmations can be life-changing.

Burning the Victim Flag

When I take a survey of the e-mails I've received, the posts I see floating around the social media groups I'm in, and the general attitude online, I see one thing they all have in common. I guess it shouldn't be too surprising because I see it in almost all areas of life and in a lot of our culture.

Everywhere you look, it seems, there's a victim.

....

* Because . . . awkward!

The truth is almost all of us have the "right" to be the victim in our stories. Almost all of us have had bad stuff happen to us. We didn't ask for it. We weren't able to defend ourselves. We have a completely legit reason to let that bad stuff label us as victims. You really are allowed to play the victim card if you want.

Yep. You're allowed.

However, if you want to see success—and I'm not talking about money, but about that feeling deep down where you know you've done something amazing—and if you want to take actual steps into the life you imagine for your family, you're going to have to put down that flag and burn it. You won't forget what happened to you, and you can still tell your story, but you will have to forget about using it as an excuse not to reach your potential.

You want to be great? Burn the victim flag.

Some of the most amazing stories I have heard are of people who refused to let their victim status define their lives. Every Nike commercial ever is about that very thing. And I'm going to go out on a limb and say that every successful person I have known has stepped away from a victim status that they have every right to declare. They have taken a match to their victim flags.

In my Boss Up Facebook group, a common and resounding issue is that many of us are not taking responsibility for our businesses. There's always someone else to point the finger at:

- "I didn't grow this month because my partner didn't do her part."
- "I didn't get enough interaction on my Facebook; that's why I'm not growing."
- "She doesn't spend enough time with me."
- "She won't write me back, so everybody hates what I'm doing."
- "They hurt my feelings, so I'm done."
- "I don't know how to make graphics, so I can't sell my products."

I could go on, and I bet you money that you have heard one of these or something like it and found yourself rolling your eyes. We can recognize the self-pity in others, and yet we tell ourselves the same lies. We act the part of victims in our stories because it's easier that way. It's more comfortable to blame others or our circumstances or our lack of growth than to say, "I just didn't get it done" or "I just didn't try something new" or "I'm believing my own lies about my effort."

I know you're tired of the complaints and the drama and the whining and the blaming and the victim status. I know I am. So why are we allowing ourselves to be that way?

I'm talking to me too. Believe me, peeps, I'm not immune to that temptation to play the victim. I learned from a young age how to get what I wanted because nobody was going to give it to me. Some bad stuff happened in my life that nobody knew about, and then I got a little older and more bad stuff happened to me. There were a lot of years when I was bitter and straight up mad about it. And believe me, I flew that victim flag high.*

You know what though? I'm thankful now for all the bad stuff that happened to me. It made me tough in a few places (not all, mind you) that a lot of people aren't. I learned how to get stuff done. I learned to try new things. I learned how to work really hard. I learned that there is power in my pain. And I also learned that no amount of babying myself for the bad stuff that happened can fix the past or make me better in the present.

So I've decided that I'm not a victim. I'm a badass.

It's time we end this victim drama. It's time to burn the flags. Let's take responsibility. Let's assume everything happening in our business is 100 percent our responsibility (even if it is not). Let's do whatever we have to do to point the finger inward rather than shaking it at someone else.

What can *you* do right now to fix the issues? What can *you* do right now to create some excitement? What can *you* do to spread magic?

When you burn that victim flag, you'll find that you love your job so much more, and you'll feel so much more fulfilled when you reach your goals. You will still be pointing that finger inward, but now it will mean something different.

You did that. Look at what you did! You are amazing. You are a badass.

....

* You guys, I practically planned downtown parades in my sad honor. I can't believe people are still friends with me after college.

So from this day on, you and I—we're not going to wallow in our victim status. We're going to call that stuff on the carpet, guys. We're going to be our own solutions. We're not going to wait on other people to solve our issues or do enough. We're going to make hard choices, going to put ourselves out there, have hard conversations and earn our place as the heroes of our stories.

Because we're women.

Because it's what we do.

Refusing to Fail

When you own your own business, the only person who can fire you is you. The only way you can fail at your dreams is to quit on them before you reach the finish line.

If you're in a place where you think, *That's it. I am done with this. I'll just choose another lifelong dream to follow,* it's time to choose a new way to get to there. You don't abandon the thing you feel like you're supposed to be doing with your life. If this is your purpose, you have to stick it out. You just need to change the vehicle to get you there if you can't make the first one work.

Chances are you'll reach one or more points on your road to achieving your goals when you're convinced that you've had enough. Things just aren't going the way you planned. All you can see around you at the moment is disappointment and failure. You can't remember why you went into business in the first place, and all you can think about at the moment is getting out.

And you can do that, of course. You're a grown woman and your own boss, which means that giving up is a choice you can make. There may even be legitimate reasons to leave your business and choose another course. But fear isn't one of them. Frustration isn't one of them. Failure isn't one of them. Don't give up on pursuing your dream unless your dream has really changed, unless you've thought long and hard and finally decided you want something else out of your life.

Even then, before you make that decision to quit, I challenge you to do the following:

1. **Remember your ikigai.** When you first started, you were unstoppable. Ask yourself, *Where did that girl go?*
2. **Consider how can you switch up the way you're working** to allow you to still reach your ultimate goal without doing the thing that is threatening to make you quit your life's work.
3. **Get curious about what specifically is creating this frustrated feeling in you.** Is it something you can change, avoid, move away from, or find a workaround?
4. **Ask yourself if you have done everything in your power to make what you're doing work?** Is it possible you're quitting too soon?
5. **Think about what's going to happen next?** Do you have a plan? Is the idea of something different beckoning you like a shiny thing on the horizon? (Never abandon your dreams for a shiny thing.)
6. **Decide to quit tomorrow.** Tell yourself today is not the day. You need to think on it longer. You need to seek out wise counsel. Both starting and quitting are big decisions that require a lot of thought. Don't make them lightly!

Your desires, passions, and dreams deserve a relentless effort on your part. Don't be that girl who switches her "thing" every week, month, or year. We all know that person who has a new dream every other month, and we can never keep up with what she's doing now. Each time she starts something new, she goes all in, but then within months her desire for that thing fades, and she's on to the next shiny thing that's going to help her build a business and a significant life. I see this all the time with work-at-home businesses. People switch from product to product, idea to idea, always thinking the next one is what will make them rich. No wonder their businesses never get off the ground. They're not willing to stick to an enterprise long enough for it to succeed. Or maybe they're just unwilling to work hard enough for it to happen.

But I'm not like that, and neither are you. We are not soft, delicate flowers who can't hack the hard stuff. We're not going to accept that walking away from a dream is the right choice just because the going gets hard. We're hardcore business owners who work our tails off to grab onto the life we've always dreamed about. We're here to break cycles and create a beautiful life for ourselves and our family.

Here's the thing about your business, friends. You can refuse to fail at this. If you resolve to become successful and achieve significance as a business owner, you can do that, but first you're going to have to take *quit* out of the multiple-choice options. You have to stop hanging onto your Plan B.

Look, I'm realistic. Failure is going to be a part of your business—and if you're doing it right it will be a very large part. A lot of things you try are going to turn out horrible, like ugly-cry horrible. There will be times when you fall flat on your face. But you can end up learning tremendous lessons as a result, and if you learn you haven't really failed.

For example, I had to fail at getting buy-in on a new project among a group of women, leaving them scared to death and literally crying over what I'd shared. I had to do a ton of damage control and firefighting because of that failure, but it taught me a lesson about how to be more delicate and considerate of emotions so as not to scare or freak others out at the buy-in stage.

Failure is only a waste if you don't learn from it the first time. And that happens, of course. How many people do you know who trip over a bump in the road and then continue to trip on the same bump again and again? Can they not see what's happening?

I recently talked to a woman who has made the same mistakes almost her entire life, but she cannot see that because she's too close to the problem, and she pushes away the people who tell her the truth. She needs to learn that one of her greatest assets is the fresh perspective of someone who will tell her the truth with love. Actually, that's true for all of us.

Refusing to fail doesn't mean that we never experience failure. There's no success that doesn't come after crushing failure upon crushing failure. But we can choose to "fail up" without giving up. Failure doesn't mean it's the right time to call it quits on your dream.

This week Michael and I had a contractor out working on our

basement, and that contractor said the most profound thing to me. He said, "Hard work isn't something this industry is drowning in, which I'm thankful for because that means more for us."

Again—slow clap.

More for us.

Yes!

In any business or venture you must come to a place where only the strong are going to survive. You must. As painful as it is, if you don't have to work for it, you just won't make it. Doing something great requires greatness within, and that's not handed out for free. I wish it was, but it isn't.

Some people are going to sabotage their success for whatever reason, and that's not something you can control. You can only control you.

Most people are going to quit on a dream when it gets really hard. They'll decide it's not what they really want. They'll change their minds about what they're willing to sacrifice to get there.

If it was easy, everyone would be their own boss. True entrepreneurs are rare because entrepreneurship is really hard. But you can do it. You can refuse to fail. When other people walk away, they're just laying a path for your growing success. When your competitors quit, you'll be there to swoop in.

If your business is your ikigai, you won't be able to walk away easily. You'll need it in your life like I do, and I need my business like I need air. It's what I puffy-heart love. There's no amount of failure that can make me give up on the dream. I'm so emotionally connected to this product, service, or opportunity that I'll find a way to make it work.

This is a mind-set, and it definitely takes strength of mind. If you're doing it right, you're leaving it all on the table at the end of your workday. You're also setting yourself up to do really hard things that you haven't done in the past so that you can learn new things. And you're doing all that right in the middle of the rest of your life.

If you're like me and working from home, for instance, you will have kids walking in and out during the day, vying for your attention. I can't stress enough how hard it is to be stretched between a to-do list and kids who need another snack.

In fact, my kids are part of the reason I do what I do. If they're going to learn to stick out the hard stuff, my kids need to see me go first. I want them to learn the lessons I've learned about goals and work and failing up and refusing to quit.

I also do what I do because I believe the world needs what I have to offer—not just the products I have to offer but the teaching and the life experience and the encouragement. And guess what? The world needs what you have to offer too. Your art. Your hand-sewn creations. Your photography skills. Your organizational savvy.

The world needs you. As I see it, that's reason enough never to give up on making your dreams a reality.

You are strong enough.

You are smart enough.

Everything you need is at your fingertips. You just need to set goals, work hard, and refuse to fail at it.

Conclusion

WHAT TO DO WITH OPINIONS, INSECURITIES, AND FEARS

I f you're going to take a chance on a new business, you're going to catch some heat for it. People will find a way to tear you down over it. (You know this already from being a mom.) This has nothing to do with you and everything to do with other people's insecurities. Taking on a new business is a risk, and it makes a lot of people uncomfortable.

To keep this reality from getting you down, I suggest you take a page from the celebrity playbook and quit reading your own press. If owning your business is what's in your heart and soul, you can't say no just because your neighbor's friend's cousin thinks it's insane. So don't listen to the neighbor's friend's cousin's opinions. Keep your head down, keep on grinding away, and make sure you wave as you pass them on your way to success.

In the face of obstacles and discouragement, many people shrink away. You will not do this. You will not hang your head low and begin to be less—that's exactly what those haters want. You will not believe other people's lies and thoughts as the truth. You will not play it safe and only do what other people think is right for you.

You will step up to the challenge. Lift your head high. Lean into the messy part. Prove them wrong with your actions.

Other people may quit, but you owe it to yourself to stick it out. You owe it to your family, who has sacrificed their time with you to allow you to chase your dream. You owe it to the people you will serve with your products and your services.

Your greatest opportunity will come when everyone else gives up. Be the one who lasts the longest. Each time a competitor gives up on herself, take that as the encouragement you need to push forward through the hard times. Yes, you will work with the clients the competitor is giving up. Yes, you will serve those clients and make them a part of your tribe. Yes, you will keep going and step into the person God made you to be.

So this is where I leave you, friends—well, at least as far as this book is concerned. It's time to *boss up* and get some stuff done. I'll be here on the sideline cheering you on in my loudest voice. You have this in the bag. Go. Do. Mess up. Start again.

Success is there waiting for you, and you're going to get there right on time.

THE *BOSS UP!* SUMMARY CHEAT SHEET FOR BUSY MOMTREPRENEURS

So you want to post about what you're learning, but writing copy isn't your strength (yet)? I got you, boo. Here you'll find both book and chapter summaries to help you turn what you're learning into bite-size pieces to share with your tribe.

Boss Up! in a Few Words

Boss Up! will prepare you to launch your business into the stratosphere by covering the fundamentals. Lindsay Teague Moreno tells her story of building personal wealth through her ten success philosophies that will have you laughing, crying, blushing, and clapping while you learn. This is the book your business has been missing.

Boss Up! in a Few More Words

Boss Up! is the answer for the momtrepreneur who's constantly running out of dry shampoo and patience. You've got a dream, but you've also got small humans who won't stop asking for a snack.

Lindsay Teague Moreno tells her story of going from stay-at-home mom to multimillion-dollar-producing entrepreneur in the raw, straight-shooting style you've been searching for. She's going to teach you the ten philosophies that have made her businesses successful and make you laugh, cry, blush, and fist-pump along the way.

Every business owner should have a copy in her office.

Chapter 1

As mothers, we have a tendency to value and nurture the hopes, dreams, and desires of our families over our own. There's a pressure to do everything and be everything for our kids while we let our passions pass with the time. In chapter 1, Lindsay gives *Boss Up!* readers the permission to be spectacular moms while also giving time and attention to the dreams of their hearts.

Chapter 2

In chapter 2 of *Boss Up!*, Lindsay shares the story of what led her to become a millionaire mama while staying at home with her three little girls. As a mom, admitting that her role as a mother wasn't fulfilling her life dreams was tough and shame-filled—until she ripped off the Band-Aid and stepped into her purpose as a momtrepreneur. If you've ever felt this way, you're not alone, and Lindsay is about to prove it to you.

Chapter 3

If you're the woman who has forgotten what your skills, talents, and passions are, you need chapter 3 of *Boss Up!* Lindsay walks you through a few exercises to drill down what you're good at and what you love to do. It's time to remember the entrepreneur buried inside you because she deserves a shot at her dreams.

Chapter 4

It's not enough to just think about the product or service you'd like to sell. You need to take some foundational action so you're prepared for the mess business ownership is about to throw you. In chapter 4 of *Boss Up!*, Lindsay shares the importance of thinking long-term about what you want out of and for your business. This chapter is filled with brainstorming questions and fill-in-the-blank sections so you can build your dream on a rock-solid foundation.

Chapter 5

In the world of social media perfection, having the guts to be unapologetically authentic flies in the face of our culture. You don't need a perfect house with perfectly behaved children and size 2 jeans to get attention. What you need is to give your customers something to believe in, something to trust—imperfection. In chapter 5 of *Boss Up!*, Lindsay shines a light on the importance of building an authentic tribe.

Chapter 6

Our brains are hardwired to respond to stories and feelings, yet so many entrepreneurs are focused on shoving their product information down the throats of their customers without giving time to the things that create sales and momentum. In chapter 6, Lindsay walks *Boss Up!* readers through the storytelling process and explains how they can get their customers to feel what they feel about their products.

Chapter 7

Confusing your customer is the fastest way to let your product or service die before it ever gets off the ground. In chapter 7 of *Boss Up!*, Lindsay explains brand consistency and why showing up the same way for your customer every day is the key to making the sale and creating sticky customers.

Chapter 8

In traditional sales, you find a way to convince the customer to say yes to your product by laying on pressure and making him or her say no to you over and over and over. In chapter 8 of *Boss Up!*, Lindsay demonstrates how putting the customer's needs first and presenting real value creates loyalty, trust, and a tribe that becomes your advocate.

Chapter 9

Nobody is inspired by the people who are constantly complaining about their lives. We unfollow them all the time, don't we? There's enough negativity and dissension in the world, and your complaints may garner attention, but is it the right kind of attention? In chapter 9 of *Boss Up!*, you learn how to create a positive work environment that attracts customers like a magnet.

Chapter 10

The quickest way to destroy your business is to believe you have it all figured out. Entrepreneurship is the process of constantly learning, unlearning, changing your mind, innovating, and sharing ideas. In chapter 10 of *Boss Up!*, you learn the importance of standing on the shoulders of giants and being adaptable to a new way of thinking.

Chapter 11

In order for you to connect with your customers, they need to know you and your heart behind your business. Heart-led companies have figured out how to build a common bond with their customers and translate that into sales numbers. In chapter 11 of *Boss Up!*, Lindsay walks you through understanding why you do what you do and how to share it with the world.

Chapter 12

Many new entrepreneurs miss a lot of details when building their businesses. In chapter 12 of *Boss Up!*, readers begin to understand how important things like business licenses, insurance, contracts, and hard conversations are to the success of their businesses. Lindsay takes out all the guesswork about what you need to do to prepare your business for long-term growth, even if it's uncomfortable.

Chapter 13

As an entrepreneur, you'll quickly find out that quitting is the easiest option on some days. If you're emotionally connected to your product or service and you've created a path to the kind of success you want, quitting won't be on the table for you. In chapter 13 of *Boss Up!*, you learn how to create the kinds of goals that inspire action and keep you moving forward, even on the hardest days.

ACKNOWLEDGMENTS

A.K.A. This book would still be sitting in my brain without the following people.

Before I thank anyone else, I want to recognize the sacrifice that my family made that allows this book to be in your hands.

Michael Moreno, so many men would not sit back and give their wives the time and support to walk through this entire book process. From the initial idea and concept meetings, to the groundwork, proposal creation, interviews, decisions, rollercoaster emotions, time to write, time to edit, and the rework process, you've done it all with love and the most support of any person in my life. I say it all the time, and I mean it: this is worth the labor only if you're by my side to see the reward. Thank you. I love you so much. It almost feels wrong to be so in love with someone. Bust out the Amos Lee, a bottle of 2010 Brunello, and let's celebrate!

Teagan Elizabeth, Boston Diane, and Kennedy Elise, you girls are so loved in the deepest part of my soul. I hope you all know that everything I do is to show you how much more is inside of you. I often imagine what I would do if I was faced with the ability to go back in time and relive a moment with each of you. I think I'd choose sitting on the empty floor, eating Chinese food on paper plates, playing board games, and sleeping next to each other in the master bedroom of our brand-new Barbie Dream House. I love our life together, and I am so grateful that I have you three to share it with. Thank you for the time apart to write and make this book a reality. I love you three so much.

Next I want to thank Mike Salisbury, my agent, for molding me into an author. I am so thankful to have you in my corner and on my team. Mike, I could not and would not want to do this without you to guide me. Thank you for the prayers, support, effort, and time. I hope this book does the work you've put into me justice. Michael and I owe you and Amy an Avalanche game in CO soon.

To the entire Yates & Yates family, thanks for taking a chance on me and on momtrepreneurs. I am so lucky to have the best literary agency in the business. Matt and Heidi, we had so much fun here in Denver with you guys; let's do that again.

Megan Dobson and Daisy Hutton (my publishers), the day I talked to you and the rest of the W team on the phone before Boss Up married HarperCollins, I knew you were the right choice. Not because of the other authors you publish (What's up Joanna Gaines?). Not because of the talent on the team (*talent* isn't a strong enough word). Not because of the money. Not because I had to. Not even because I like to listen to your Southern accents. It was because of the people—because of you! I felt peace about saying yes to W because I knew I liked you—I wanted to be your friend. You can never go wrong when you bet on people. I'm the luckiest author to ever live to have my book grace the shelves of your office. Thank you for believing in me.

Megan, I want to shout out a special thank you to you for helping me whittle down the content in *Boss Up!* You really did help me keep the very best words in the book, just like Mike said you would. You are the secret sauce, my friend. Every author should have a Megan to care for her book. Thank you.

To the rest of the HarperCollins/Thomas Nelson/W team, you guys are superstars, and I appreciate you caring for *Boss Up!* and working so hard on getting it into the hands of the people who need it. Paula Major (editorial), Kristi Smith, Denise George, Ashley Reed, Kimberly Golladay, Kristen Andrews, and Lori Lynch, you are an integral part of making *Boss Up!* happen, and I couldn't wish for a better team in my corner. Thank you. Thank you. Thank you.

To my inner circle/ride-or-die friends. Guys! Look at this. Your name is in the back of a second book. You've supported me through this twice (soon to be three times), and I am so glad to have a friend group that has more interest in loving me than competing with me. It's so rare. Kelly Block, Liz Bienas, Melissa Koehler, Leah Friedman, Janell Vonigas, and Carrie Hoener, you all have a permanent place in my heart. Thank you for your time, advice, support, hand-holding, laughter, tears, girls' trips, late-night texts, phone calls, and real talk. Crossing my fingers for NYC in September.

Liz Bienas, thank you for the wordsmithing, idea bouncing, never-ending to-do list-making and ceaseless help you give me. You are so important not only to my business but also to me. I love you.

Kelly Block, you were the first person to make it through the ridiculously long version of this book and give me feedback. You're the person I turn to when I'm (insert any heightened emotion) and I need a girlfriend. Thank you for hanging in with me through the last twenty years. I love you.

Yoshika Green, thank you for being so brilliant when it comes to the written word (and gospel music) and for your encouragement. Your review of this book gave me life when I was so uncertain. I appreciate you, and I'm so excited to see our friendship develop.

To my fourth-grade teacher, Mrs. Kortman, I lived for creative writing in your class. You were the teacher who led me to one of my great loves twenty-eight years ago: writing. Your impact on my life lives on today. Thank you.

Last, but certainly not least, to my tribe. Thank you for supporting what I do. Thanks for coming to the events, listening to the podcasts, buying the books, bringing me to speak to your people, reading the posts, joining the groups, and sharing my words with others. *Boss Up!* is both for you and because of you. You have changed my life in the most profound way. You allow me to live in my purpose. You are everything, and you accept me, flaws and all. I'm in your corner cheering you on. Thank you.

NOTES

Chapter 1: The "Right Kind" of Mom

1. The term *lawnmower parent* went viral in late 2018 after a viral post on an online community for teachers. See "Lawnmower Parents Are the New Helicopter Parents and We Are Not Here for It," We Are Teachers (website), August 30, 2018, https://www.weareteachers.com/lawnmower -parents/?fbclid=IwAR3YAXr1CgrIXGdymuxx5umSZxHjib5 16i-LjSSfq-NpBjBZhCzkBdBh8NM.

Chapter 4: Success Philosophy #1: Think Long-Term

1. Stephen R. Covey, *The 7 Habits of Highly Effective People: Powerful Lessons in Personal Change,* 25th anniversary ed. (New York: Simon & Schuster, 2004, orig. pub. 1989), 102–153. See also "Habit 2: Begin with the End in Mind," FranklinCovey: The Ultimate Competitive Advantage (website), https://www.franklincovey.com/the-7-habits/habit-2.html.

2. Jared Dees, "The Grunt Test (Donald Miller and StoryBrand)," Jared Dees (website), January 18, 2018, http://jareddees.com/grunt-test/.

3. To do this, go to https://www.uspto.gov/trademarks-application-process /search-trademark-database.

4. Barbara Farfan, "Learn About Apple's Mission Statement," The Balance, Small Business, December 24, 2017, https://www.thebalancesmb.com /apple-mission-statement-4068547.

Chapter 5: Success Philosophy #2: Be Unapologetically Yourself

1. Lance Armstrong with Sally Jenkins, *It's Not about the Bike: My Journey Back to Life* (New York: Putnam Adult, 2000).

2. Mahita Gajanan, "A Restaurant Crowd Jeered Lance Armstrong, So He Bought Everyone's Meals," *Time*, July 26, 2018, http://time.com/5349720 /lance-armstrong-restaurant-boos/.

3. Scott Davis, "Why Lance Armstrong's Brand Is Beyond Repair," *Forbes*, January 17, 2013, https://www.forbes.com/sites/scottdavis/2013/01/17 /getting-lanced-why-lance-armstrongs-brand-is-beyond- repair/#5d4462371f33.

Chapter 6: Success Philosophy #3: Tell Stories and Connect Through Feeling

1. Donald Miller, *Scary Close: Dropping the Act and Finding True Intimacy* (Nashville: Nelson Books, 2014).

2. Donald Miller, *Building a StoryBrand: Clarify Your Message So Customers Will Listen* (Nashville: HarperCollins Leadership, 2017), Kindle.

3. Miller, *Building a StoryBrand,* chapters 2 and 3, adapted.

4. Simon Sinek, "How Great Leaders Inspire Action," TED video, 17:58, filmed September 2009, at the TEDxPuget Sound event in Newcastle, WA, https://www.ted.com/talks/simon_sinek_how_great_leaders_inspire _action?language=en.

5. Sinek, *Start with Why: How Great Leaders Inspire Everyone to Take Action* (New York: Penguin/Portfolio, 2009).

6. Phillip Adcock, *Master Your Brain* (New York: Sterling Publishing, 2015).

7. Dan Hill, *Emotionomics: Leveraging Emotions for Business Success*, 2nd ed. (Philadelphia: Kogan Page, 2010), 19.

Chapter 8: Success Philosophy #5: Use the Unsales Tactic

1. Mark Suster, "How to Identify Client Pain Points," *Inc.,* June 17, 2013, https://www.inc.com/mark-suster/how-to-identify-client-pain-points.html.

2. Suster, "How to Identify."

3. Brené Brown, "Empathy Has No Script," 10th Human Consulting, LLC (website), January 25, 2017.

4. Ron Dicker, "Cards Against Humanity Actually RAISES Prices on Black Friday, *Huffpost*, December 3, 2013, https://www.huffingtonpost.com /2013/12/03/cards-against-humanity-black-friday-raise-price_n_4379357 .html.

5. Laura Stampler, "Why This Company Sent Poop to 30,000 People for Black Friday," *Time,* December 15, 2014, http://time.com/3634443/cards-against -humanity-poop-black-friday/.

6. Matt Weinberger, "This Game Company Made $71,145 on Black Friday by Selling Nothing for $5 a Pop," *Business Insider,* November 29, 2015, https://www.businessinsider.com/cards-against-humanity-made-71145-on-black-friday-2015-11.

7. Reed Alexander, "Black Friday Stunt Convinces People to Donate $1000,000 for 'Holiday Hole,'" CNN, November 28, 2016, https://www.cnn.com/2016/11/28/us/holiday-hole-cards-against-humanity-black-friday-trnd/index.html.

8. Mix, "CAH's Fake Super Bowl Ad Was Actually a Brilliant Marketing Stunt," NW (website), February 6, 2017, https://thenextweb.com/creativity/2017/02/06/carads-humanity-super-bowl-ad/.

9. For more information about these ventures, see https://www.ltmstock.com/ and https://www.thebossupshop.com/.

Chapter 9: Success Philosophy #6: Put on Your Positive Pants

1. Rachel Premack, "17 Seriously Disturbing Facts About Your Job," *Business Insider,* August 2, 2018, https://www.businessinsider.com/disturbing-facts-about-your-job-2011-2.

2. Check out Shawn Achor's TED talk called "The Happy Secret to Better Work" (filmed May 14, 2011, at the TEDxBloomington event in Bloomington, IN, https://www.ted.com/talks/shawn_achor_the_happy_secret_to_better_work?language=en), and his book, *The Happiness Advantage: How a Positive Brain Fuels Success in Work and Life* (New York: Penguin/Crown, 2010).

3. "*Saving Private Ryan* (1998) Quotes," imdb.com (website), accessed December 11, 2018, https://www.imdb.com/title/tt0120815/quotes/?tab=qt&ref_=tt_trv_qu.

4. Dalai Lama Center for Peace and Education, "Shawn Achor: The Happiness Advantage," summary of Shawn Achor's presentation at Heart-Mind Conference 2013, Vancouver, Canada, https://dalailamacenter.org/heart-mind-2013-helping-children-thrive/heart-mind-2013-presenters/shawn-achor.

Chapter 10: Success Philosophy #7: Keep Learning

1. Malcolm Gladwell, quoted in Maria Popova, "Malcolm Gladwell on Criticism, Tolerance, and Changing Your Mind," Brain Pickings (blog), June 24, 2014, https://www.brainpickings.org/2014/06/24/malcolm-gladwell-nypl-interview/.

Chapter 11: Success Philosophy #8: Understand Your Why

1. Rob Bell, "How to Reboot Your Life with the Japanese Philosophy of *Ikigai*," YouTube video, 7:02, April 2018, https://www.youtube.com /watch?v=2Ym5ikl45Ww.

Chapter 12: Success Philosophy #9: Treat Your Business Like a Business

1. Bernard B. Kamoroff, *475 Tax Deductions for Businesses and Self-Employed Individuals: An A-to-Z Guid to Hundreds of Tax Write-Offs*, 13th ed. (Guildford, CT: Lyons Press, 2019). Note: This book has been in print a long time and gone through many editions as the tax laws change. Be sure to reference the latest one.

Chapter 13: Success Philosophy #10: Set Goals + Work Hard + Refuse to Fail

1. Aastha Atray Banan, "'Never Give Yourself a Plan B,' Advices [sic] Lego House Singer Ed Sheeran," *Hindustan Times*, March 7, 2015, https://www .hindustantimes.com/brunch/never-give-yourself-a-plan-b-advices-lego -house-singer-ed-sheeran/story-WePkdm8RY10ECtEWJrRJMO.html.
2. Jennie Allen, "Paralyzed in the Name of Humility," Jennie Allen (blog), April 29, 2015, https://www.jennieallen.com/paralyzed-in-the-name-of -humility/.

ABOUT THE AUTHOR

Lindsay Teague Moreno is an author, podcaster, and owner of three multimillion-dollar-producing businesses. In her perfect world, Internet baby goat videos flow freely, mornings start at 10 a.m., and the word *play-date* is stricken from the English language. Also, if it's not too much to ask, dry shampoo is free, and the dishwasher loads itself.

In just two short years, Lindsay built a seven-figure personal income using only social media. She did this with three little girls at home and all the mom duties that come along with it. Raising businesses and babies at the same time is no easy feat, but anything is possible if you have enough dry shampoo and wine.

Lindsay's writing is straight-shooting, raw, and real. Much of her drive to succeed comes from tragic personal loss and the hard knocks experienced in life. No stranger to failure, Lindsay is not afraid to speak out about challenging topics. Her ability to be vulnerable while making people laugh is why so many females are drawn to her content. Lindsay doesn't beat around the bush when it comes to the hard stuff.

Her previous Amazon bestselling book, *Getting Noticed*, is a road map of how she grew several businesses online from scratch. CNBC and *Entrepreneur* featured Lindsay's sales business, which is projected to bring in $300 million in 2019, and has grown to a team of more than 525,000 members in five years using social media.

Never in the history of ever has someone been more allergic to the feel-good fluff that most entrepreneurs and speakers put out as content. Whether reading Lindsay's blog posts, social media feeds, or books, you'll get real advice for getting out of your own way and starting, growing, and scaling businesses. Get ready to start turning your dreams into reality.

Momtrepreneurs, listen up! You don't have time for another change-everything-you're-doing-on-social-media-and-be-just-like-me book. You need information, and you need it fast.

Lindsay Teague Moreno is one of the smartest, most insightful people I've ever met when it comes to getting noticed. I read this, not just because I wanted to endorse it, but because I needed it. Don't miss this!

JON ACUFF, *NEW YORK TIMES* **BESTSELLING AUTHOR / SPEAKER**

getting
NOTICED

a no-nonsense guide to **standing out** and **selling more** for momtrepreneurs who "ain't got time for that"

lindsay teague moreno

Do you want to grow your following, sell more product, and experience the freedom that comes with being your own boss? *Getting Noticed* isn't the secret to social media; it's a no-fluff, take charge guide to the way we present ourselves and our businesses and connect with customers online.

AVAILABLE NOW!!!

ISBN: 9781944298159 (softcover) 9781721384884 (Audio)

© Brooke Austin

CONNECT WITH ME

Find me online and dig deeper into building and expanding your business.

Instagram: @lindsayteague
Facebook Page: @lindsayteague
Facebook Group: The Boss Up Community
My email: hello@lindsaytm.com
My website: lindsaytm.com
Podcast: Boss Up Podcast
Pinterest: @lindsayteague